IDLE THOUGHTS

IDLE THOUGHTS

STUART DORRANCE

© Stuart Dorrance, 2017

Published by Madbox Publishing

All rights reserved. No part of this book may be reproduced, adapted, stored in a retrieval system or transmitted by any means, electronic, mechanical, photocopying, or otherwise without the prior written permission of the author.

The rights of Stuart Dorrance to be identified as the author of this work have been asserted in accordance with the Copyright, Designs and Patents Act 1988.

A CIP catalogue record for this book is available from the British Library.

ISBN 978-0-9955811-0-4

Book layout and cover design by Clare Brayshaw

Photographs by Mark Brooks
Photographic Design by Samantha Dorrance

Prepared and printed by:

York Publishing Services Ltd
64 Hallfield Road
Layerthorpe
York YO31 7ZQ

Tel: 01904 431213

Website: www.yps-publishing.co.uk

DEDICATION

To Mum, Dad, Karen, Samantha & Kurt

CONTENTS

Introduction	xii
Why does everyone rush about?	1
Watching the birds (poem)	4
Why you should never invite a guitarist	5
The day I rushed my pet rabbit to the vets	8
Why Jack Russells are crackers	11
Your landline number has been randomly selected	14
Kennel life	18
Thousands of kennels (poem)	20
Don't kill yourself, have a Mars bar	21
Going for a walk with the dog	25
You don't have to grow up if you don't want to	28
Summer is the worst time of the year	31
Why worry today, when you can worry tomorrow?	35
Why worry today (poem)	39

Can I go back in time and make a name for myself please?	40
Forced fun	44
Playing-out is the new playing-in	47
Isn't winter wonderful?	50
If you like DIY so much, then why don't you smile?	53
Get it right in the first place?	56
Have you married a snorer?	60
Taking myself off to thousands of magical worlds	63
Going to bed (poem)	65
Healthy food anyone?	66
It's not food, it's polyfilla	70
Don't listen, chocolate is smaller	73
Making the most out of your council tax	76
Technology in the wrong hands	79
Get rid of clutter, sort out your breadbin	82
What is it with signs?	86
In bed with my wife	90
Ambushed by the dogs trust mob	93
What's the big fascination with celebrities?	97
School is bad for your education	100
It's your classroom (poem)	102
Shall we all get dressed up and pretend?	103

What I do in public toilets	107
We've been here how long?	110
The perils of knocking on a bit	113
Don't be fooled by the smiling woman in a bowling t-shirt	116
Can we have our fields back please?	119
Do you want any help with your packing?	122
Fancy an expensive day out?	125
I'm sick to the back teeth of enthusiasts	129
Going on my NHS apple hunt	132
What's the fascination of nesting in Walsall?	135
Don't waste time doing something that doesn't need doing	138
Busy doing nothing (poem)	142
Smile, you're on camera	143
Having a yearly hip check	146
Don't be fooled by Valentine's Day	149
I'm not killing the planet, honest	152
Having a wash should not be a chore	155
I'm never on my own because I'm with me	159
In a world on my own (poem)	161
How to survive in a scutter town	162
Trying to work out the best way to clean my teeth	165

Is it a train station or the starship enterprise?	168
Buy now and pay later	171
Going to the doctors but only if you know what's wrong with you	174
He can ride a bike, give him a gong	180
Get yourself a bar of pharmacological activity	183
The best way to look after your guts	186
What's not on television tonight?	189
Animals don't need chemists do they?	192
Why plaster wrappers are life threatening	195
Don't talk people's heads off	198
Appreciate what you already have	201
Why wearing skinny jeans can kill you	204
Why I think exercising is bad for you	207
They don't want work do they?	210
Make up your own lists	213
Why do we do that?	215

INTRODUCTION

You buy a book, you open the cover and then you find yourself wading through pages and pages of endless drivel, before finally getting to the real reason why you bought the book in the first place.

Yes, it's the famous book introduction. That part of the book that really gets on my nerves.

Book introductions as far as I'm concerned, are totally unnecessary and just get in the way of the main event.

The thing is, if I go out and buy a book about Victorian Britain, then I actually want to read a book about Victorian Britain. I don't want to read the complete history about the author, or the reasons behind why he or she decided to write it, or how much research they had to do for it, or why they lived in Cambridge but then decided to live in North London… I'm just not interested. All I want to do is get to Chapter One and get on with it.

Reading a book introduction to me, is like having to sit through *Eastenders* before your favourite film comes on, or having to listen to the warm up act before Tom Jones comes on stage.

Basically, I just want to get straight to the action, without all the added annoyances beforehand.

A book I picked up the other day, had a thirty-page introduction in it! Thirty pages!!! Thirty pages all about the author's life, from the time he filled his last nappy, right up to the time he wrote his first novel. Thirty pages of mind-numbing information, all about himself and totally unrelated to what was actually written on the front cover.

You won't have to worry about that with this introduction though, because the title on the front of this book is exactly what you will get on the inside. This means I won't be banging on about the research I've done, what inspired me to write it, what I've written in the past, or why it's taken me so long to do it.

This is simply a book of my *Idle Thoughts* by me, and my dislike for book introductions is just one of them.

WHY DOES EVERYONE RUSH ABOUT?

As I write this first chapter, I am currently sitting in a lovely café, enjoying a nice cup of coffee.

I am also taking my time with it… I don't do rushing.

Why do people constantly rush about?

Train stations are a perfect example of this. Everyone rushing around in a mad panic, because they are late for work and worried that they might miss their train.

This begs the question…

Why not go out ten minutes earlier? Or even better… Don't go out at all.

If you think about it, most the rushing about we do at work is for someone else's benefit anyway, so is it really worth all the hassle?

A friend of mine rushed about as a sales rep for a company for over two years. He was here, there and everywhere, which meant he had very little time for himself or his family.

Luckily for him though they made him redundant, which was a Godsend, because that made him go out and find something else in life that he really wanted to do. The thing is, if that hadn't have happened, then he could have ended up being there for years.

Even when people are not at work though, they just can't resist in rushing about. It's become a way of life…

When you're constantly rushing though, you tend to miss the most important things in life. You're never in the moment, because you're always thinking ahead. The trouble is, when you're always thinking ahead, you never really get to where you really want to get to.

Last week I was out and about in a very busy town centre.

As usual the town was full of rushers, all darting about from shop to shop. I wasn't though… I stopped and watched a bird collect a few twigs for its nest. It was a special little moment and do you know what? It was all mine.

There I was, in a busy shopping precinct, surrounded by thousands of people, all rushing here, there and everywhere, but did anybody else notice the bird? No… Nobody… Just me.

Then I looked up and saw two wood pigeons sitting on the branch of a tree. They looked so content as they sat there, casually looking around. But did anyone else notice them? No.

What about the trees, the clouds, all the old buildings, the pigeon eating a sandwich?

What about the butterflies on the hanging basket, or the sparrows taking cover in a hawthorn bush? Did anybody notice them? No.

The trouble is, people are far too busy to notice anything THAT important. Everyone is focused on going to work, going to the shops, getting home and then watching the television.

The thing is, you're not going to be around in a hundred years' time, so you may as well stand back and take it all in now.

If I go to the shops, I don't just go to the shops… I'll park up, bring down my drawbridge and take in what's around me.

There may be a cat on a wall. There may be a couple of birds having a bath in a puddle. I may spot a squirrel scurrying up a tree. I may just look at the tree. It doesn't really matter what's there or what's around me, there's always something to take in.

What I'm trying to say is… Don't rush about trying to do everything in life, because the chances are, if you do, then you'll miss everything.

Take life easy… Don't be blind to what really matters.

Take off those blinkers and look beyond this world of everyday life that everyone else calls 'normal'. Live life that is normal to you and not what is perceived to be 'normal' by everyone else. Once you do that, then you will be a more relaxed person. You will realise what a crazy, mad world we all live in and that there is no reason at all for you to be rushing about.

You will also be more aware of what's going on around you, as you come to realise your world is much more important than this one.

So as I finish my coffee, I am noting the people that are sitting around me.

Some are sitting staring at their phones, others are desperately rushing to get back out to the shops.

Me? Well, I'll just carry on looking at the beautiful tree outside and watch, as the wind gently blows through the leaves…

And why not? It is mine after all.

Watching the Birds

Watching all the birds
That no one else can see
It feels really special
That they are there just for me

I take a seat on a bench
And throw some crumbs on the floor
A bird flies from a tree
And I throw down some more

We sit and have a chat
And talk about the day
And even when it's quiet
We still have plenty to say

I sometimes take a glance
At a world that isn't mine
All busy doing nothing
But that suits me just fine

Because I'm somewhere else
I'm in a place I've always known
And may it never change
Because we like it on our own

WHY YOU SHOULD NEVER INVITE A GUITARIST

Invite a guitarist round for tea and nine times out of ten, they will turn up with a guitar thrown over their shoulder, all ready to bore the living daylights out of everyone.

Even when you think they've turned up empty-handed, they always somehow, seem to manage to find a guitar from somewhere.

It's always the same…

You're sitting there, reminiscing about old times over a nice quiet drink, when all of a sudden you notice Eric Clapton over in the corner, unzipping his guitar case.

You will find that no other instrumentalist anywhere in the world will ever do this. They will always keep their musical abilities close to their chest, but a guitarist is different. They will annoy everyone and anyone, with their constant strumming for hours.

Can you ever imagine someone getting a bassoon out halfway through the evening, or turning up with a trombone under their arm, or fetching a set of drums out of the boot? It just doesn't happen.

I went to a party the other week. We were all having a really nice time, everyone was chatting and the food was flowing.

After about 45 minutes, I bumped into an old friend of mine that I hadn't seen for quite a while. He used to work for one of the major supermarkets, but his main passion in life was music and he was a decent saxophonist back in the day. I was really curious to know if he still played.

"Have you played your saxophone recently?" I said, as I reached for my plate of sandwiches.

"I haven't played in a long while to be honest," he replied. "I've been learning the guitar for the last twelve months though."

All of a sudden, I felt a cold shiver shoot down the back of my spine. I had already started planning my exit and thinking up excuses for why I needed to leave. Leaving early had all of a sudden become a major priority, as it was just a matter of time, before Eric Clapton would soon be giving us his rendition of 'Stairway to Heaven'.

Suddenly, as if by magic, a guitar appeared around his neck and before I had chance to slip my coat on and make a quick exit, I was being given a rendition of 'Honky Tonk Women' by the Rolling Stones (played very badly may I add) by an old friend, who I was very quickly beginning to despise.

The room had now become silent.

All conversations between various parties had ground to a complete halt, as eyes had now become transfixed on the manic guitarist, standing next to me.

The trouble is, guitarists think that people actually enjoy listening to what they are playing, but the truth is they don't. People would much rather chat, eat or just sit and have a peaceful drink.

So if you're thinking about having a party in the near future, here's some sound advice to help it run smoothly.

1) Under no circumstances should you invite anyone who plays a guitar, anyone who is learning to play a guitar or even anyone that owns a guitar, because I can guarantee that everyone will know about it within ten minutes of their arrival.

2) As a precautionary measure you should remove any guitars that you have in the house beforehand, just in case a rogue guitarist turns up that you were unaware of.

Taking these simple steps, will hopefully ensure your party runs efficiently and will not be hijacked by the ultimate guitar party pooper.

You should also be very careful when going to visit friends too.

Calling in for what you envisaged to be an innocent cup of tea and a friendly chat, can sometimes lead to a full blown back catalogue of Hank Marvin, performed by someone who hadn't even touched a guitar last time you called round.

Unfortunately these types of encounters are unavoidable and although your visit will be painful and distressing at the time, the good thing is at least you'll know not to call round again.

Regrettably, an estimated 1.5 billion people around the world now play the guitar, which means that, unfortunately, there's never one too far away... Stay vigilant.

THE DAY I RUSHED MY PET RABBIT TO THE VETS

Having a pet and refusing to be brainwashed into having pet insurance is definitely the way forward as far as I'm concerned.

Please be prepared though for the time when your precious bundle of joy needs medical attention. This of course may never happen, but if it does, you'd better brace yourself.

Rushing your pet rabbit to the vets, late on a Friday night is not advisable, but when it's panting and its eyes are bulging, it's something that needs to be done.

Unfortunately, this is exactly the situation we found ourselves in a few years ago with our rabbit Johnny English.

He hadn't been right all day to be honest. He'd been very quiet and subdued, but unfortunately decided to wait until half past eleven at night, before going into his mini-fit.

So in the car he went and off I shot to the vets with a very distressed bunny lying on the back seat.

When I arrived and noticed that there was only me, the rabbit, the vet and the receptionist in attendance, I just knew that it was going to be an expensive night.

"Have you got pet insurance?" The receptionist asked, as she reached for a pet admission form.

"No I haven't," I replied as I clutched my poor little panting rabbit.

There was a nervous silence as she looked me up and down with an astonished frown across her face.

"Oh," she said and proceeded to fill out the form.

I could see the pound signs in her eyes as she filled in Johnny's particulars.

Following a brief examination of my poor little panting, uninsured pet, she advised me that to be on the safe side, Johnny English should stay in overnight for observation.

I was slightly concerned about this, but as he looked like he was on the verge of pegging it, thought that it was probably the best thing to do under the circumstances.

Anyway, I booked him in and headed off home.

The next morning, I telephoned the vets to find out how Johnny was doing.

"Oh he's much better this morning Mr Dorrance," she said in a very chirpy voice. "We've given him a shot of antibiotics." 'I bet you have,' I thought.

"How much do I owe you?"

"It's £155 at the moment Mr. Dorrance," came the reply. "We probably still need to keep an eye on him though, so my advice to you would be for us to keep him in for another night, just to be on the safe side." Slightly troubled by this, I asked if he would be okay to come home.

"Yes he should be fine Mr Dorrance," she replied.

That was it... I didn't need telling twice. I was out the door like a shot!

It took me exactly 15 minutes to drive there and do you know what? Within that 15 minutes, the bill had risen to £165.

"I'm so sorry about that Mr. Dorrance, but we felt Johnny needed another shot of antibiotics," she said (grinning), as she handed me the invoice.

I took a look at the situation though. What had actually happened here?

Well as far as I was concerned... Johnny had basically been given a room for the night, a room that had cost me £165 in the process. It would have been cheaper for me to book him into a Premier Inn! In fact, I could have booked a family room and we could have all stayed there. We could have had three nights away at that price, including breakfast! £165 for a night in a cage, followed by a quick shot in his left leg, doesn't really compare does it?

Looking back, I suppose £165 is a lot of money, but there again, as I've never paid pet insurance in my life, I suppose it did work out a pretty good deal

One thing's for certain though...

Next time he starts panting and pulling funny faces, I think I'll just throw some bags in the boot and we'll all clear off to Weston.

WHY JACK RUSSELLS ARE CRACKERS

First of all before I continue, let me get just one thing straight. I love dogs… They live in the moment and they are wonderful companions.

Unfortunately though, I'm not talking about dogs in this chapter. I'm talking about Jack Russell's and as far as I'm concerned, if Jack Russell's are dogs, then I'm a 22-year-old, bald, female Russian gymnast, with a twitch.

Jack Russell's are definitely one sandwich short of a picnic and if you don't believe me, then you go and spend some time with one. Take a look into a Jack Russell's eyes and you will soon come to the same conclusion. Look closely and you will soon realise that they clearly have something missing upstairs.

When they bark, they will bark for hours and hours and hours for apparently no reason whatsoever. They are erratic, uncontrollable and completely mentally unstable. There's no real getting away from it… Jack Russell's are completely bonkers!

When I lived on a housing estate in the West Midlands, I was unfortunate enough to live within one hundred yards from a Jack Russell. I always knew when the family had gone to work, because the bloody thing used to stand in the back garden and go off like a machine gun at ten barks per second for hours at a time…

But why did he do it?

People used to say that he was communicating, but who with? There was only him in the garden and as he was just standing there staring at the fence, I very much doubt it.

Let's face it… The only reason Jack Russell's bark and bark and bark is because they are completely crackers.

My mum and dad used to have a Jack Russell. They went out one day and rescued it from a dogs' home and to be honest, I'm surprised they didn't take it straight back again.

On one particular occasion, they decided to take it to Barmouth for a bit of a day out. They thought that a sleep in the car and run on the beach would do him good.

Unfortunately for my mum and dad, he barked nonstop for 120 miles and they vowed to never take him there again… Why was he barking though, and what was he barking at?

Well the truth of the matter is, nobody knows and do you know what? The Jack Russell didn't have a clue either.

I feel really sorry for people who live in Jack Russell Zones.

Jack Russell Zones are areas where Jack Russell's are allowed to plant themselves in a garden and bark nonstop all day and every day, while their selfish owners sit at work supping coffee, in the tranquillity of their workplace.

Their poor neighbours on the other hand are back at home, slowly being tortured, by the rapid machine-gun fire of the crazed mutt over the fence, with little hope of any peace for at least the next ten hours…

So what can be done about it?

Well my idea would be to introduce a bark tax monitor.

A bark tax monitor is a little device that fits to the collar, recording bark counts throughout the day. I think 10p per bark is a pretty reasonable starting point, although anyone owning a Jack Russell would very soon find themselves in the higher-rate bark tax bracket.

I think that this would be a perfect way of curbing irresponsible Jack Russell owners and, more importantly, it would bring down the noise in Jack Russell Zones across the whole of the country.

This system would definitely make a difference, and would also make people think twice, before leaving their pooch at home, annoying everyone else in the neighbourhood. That quiet coffee at work would all of a sudden not be so enjoyable, knowing that their little terror at home could quite possibly be running up hundreds, if not thousands, of pounds in barking tax.

Of course we could always try and develop a system where the tax would reduce, if the little horror was barking indoors.

This system would definitely benefit Jack Russell owners, as Jack Russell's bark nonstop where ever they are, so a tax reduction would be very much welcomed.

Another idea is to stop breeding Jack Russell's all together, with a £10,000 fine (per pup) for anyone caught breaking this rule.

This is by far my best idea and if ever elected as prime minister, I will implement it on my first day of office.

YOUR LANDLINE NUMBER HAS BEEN RANDOMLY SELECTED

You're just about to have a nice hot soak in the bath, when all of a sudden the telephone starts to ring.

You rush downstairs to answer it in anticipation of who it may be this late in the evening, but your excitement is quickly dampened, when you suddenly hear the sound of a faint voice from a far-off land, asking you if you are interested in 25 pounds worth of Marks and Spencer's gift vouchers.

When you realise that this will probably entail you travelling 55 miles and then sitting through a four-hour session of looking at pictures of an apartment that is somewhere in Bulgaria, you quickly realise that it's probably time to put the phone down.

Other times when your number is randomly selected include PPI, new windows, survey companies, accident compensation firms, free boilers and on it goes. An endless stream of companies, all trying to suck you in.

It's not only annoying companies, though.

You also have to deal with the relentless bombardment of calls by family and friends, all calling you whenever they feel like it.

The truth of the matter is, landline phones are a real pain. They are intrusive and the sooner they become obsolete the better!

You can of course remove the telephone cable from the wall socket.

This is okay if your wife isn't going to put it straight back in again, which is unfortunately what my wife tends to do.

"What if somebody's trying to call us though?" she will say, standing there with the wire in her hand. "My cousin Audrey said that she was trying to call us all day yesterday and couldn't get through."

Now if you're looking for a good enough reason to pull the telephone wire out, then you won't find a better one than that, unless you enjoy talking for over an hour and half about... Well, about nothing really. As far as I could see, this example set out by my wife just strengthened my case.

Totally fed up with all the intrusive calls and because of the insistence by my wife to keep the wire in, I decided to adopt another and much better solution... I changed the phone number AND even better, I didn't give it to anyone. This means we now have a landline that doesn't ring... Perfect!

Yes, it's true that at some point, we will receive the occasional PPI call, it's inevitable, but I'd rather have that, than get ear-bashed by a overexcited relative, rabbling on about the joys of retail shopping.

Another good reason for taking this kind of action is to use it as a sort of cleanse.

Cleanse your landline and get back some of the freedom that you once had. Put that wall between you and the banks, credit card companies, insurance companies, utility companies etc.

Cutting yourself free from these institutions is one of the most important things that you can do.

It's all about being in control, but when you're wired up to these companies (which is exactly what you are) you are far from it. You're connected and accessible to them, at any time.

Here's a perfect example…

I insist on paying my mortgage by cheque! This is fine, but if I can't get the cheque there by the due date, they will then ring me, to ask me where it is.

The trouble is, I cannot send the cheque before the due date, because then their system just thinks I am paying extra off the mortgage. It thinks the payment has been missed, so they ring me again.

Every month I had this problem of trying to explain why I always paid it a few days late, because of their inadequate computerised system.

This problem of course is no longer a problem, as ringing my old telephone number is not going to get them very far is it?

TV licensing are obviously having the same problem as well.

Their system would very often churn out our telephone number, instructing a member of staff to call, even though the overdue payment of £13.22 was just a day late.

At the end of the day, it's you who needs to be in control. It's your landline and it's you who should decide who rings it, not the bank or the credit card companies or anybody else for that matter… just you. A company can always write to you if they need to make contact.

So remember this.

If your landline number is randomly selected, just make sure it's your old one.

KENNEL LIFE

We are a population of totally bored people.
We go to work on a Monday morning, we return to our kennel on the Monday evening, we watch TV, we go to bed and then we do it all over again on Tuesday, Wednesday, Thursday and Friday.

Saturdays are just as tedious, as millions of us visit Tesco Towns to stock up on the previous week's shopping list, before rushing back to the kennel, to occupy the sofa again and prepare for hours of trash television, before setting off to bed.

Sunday is usually occupied by tidying around the kennel, washing the car, nipping to B&Q or buying some compost from the garden centre. Oh, and mowing the lawn and making a noise.

"Why does he keep saying kennel?" I hear you say. "I don't live in one?"

Well, kennel life probably hasn't seemed apparent to you before, but I can assure you, most people do live in one and the chances are, you do too.

Let me give you an insight into kennels.

Drive almost anywhere in the land and you will see rows

and rows of them, perfectly positioned, side by side, usually bunched together on what's known as a kennel estate.

Some people even share a kennel. They are called semidetached kennels.

These kennels are in fact just one kennel, that is separated by a wall on the inside and a fence on the outside. This is known as the dog run and usually gets trimmed on a Sunday.

People's hectic lives are geared towards looking after their kennel and planting themselves in it whenever possible. This is a must for almost everyone.

Every kennel is fitted with a screen too. A screen that is constantly used. This has become an integral part of kennel life.

Sometimes people will sit in the dog run, especially if the sun is out. This will result in them retiring back into their kennel, to sit in front of the screen again and munch on their favourite doggy snacks, before heading off to bed to prepare themselves to start the process all over again the next day.

Yes, this is kennel life and almost everyone lives it, no matter what size of kennel you happen to live in.

People are encouraged to get on the kennel property ladder. It is portrayed as the best option, but living in a kennel is not all it's cracked up to be. With it comes, bills, debt and entrapment.

You don't have to do it though. Yes, we all need to live somewhere, but we also need to be very careful we don't fall into the kennel trap for life.

If you're in one now, then look at it as just temporary. Don't get bogged down in a system, that wants to keep you in there forever.

At the end of the day, a man's home is his freedom, not his kennel.

Thousands of Kennels

Thousands of kennels
Lined up ten deep
They've all got a number
They're all fast asleep

They're watching the world
Through a plastic meal
They're taking it in
But it isn't real

Thousands of kennels
All playing the game
All different shapes
But exactly the same

They're ticking the boxes
They're part of the show
Thousands of kennels
With nowhere to go

DON'T KILL YOURSELF, HAVE A MARS BAR

You're driving along the motorway and you start to feel the effects of tiredness. You see a 'Tiredness Can Kill, Take a Break' sign, but you want to ignore that, because you just want to get home.

The trouble is, ignore the sign and you might not even get home, and instead of being parked up on a nice service area car park, you could very well find yourself wrapped around a tree instead.

Taking a break is definitely sound advice, but even then, a ten-minute rest is not exactly going to help you much in the tiredness stakes, because I can guarantee within 15 minutes, you will be fighting off that dreaded black silence feeling.

You may even experience the 'how the hell did I get here… I don't remember passing Junction 26?' feeling too, and if that happens then you really are in trouble.

Taking note of ways to stay safe when driving, is something you should definitely take on board, but what's the best way to stay awake when driving? Well here's some advice dished out by the so called 'experts'.

'Open a window and drink plenty of water.'

Come on… Let's get one thing straight here. Opening a window will NOT keep you awake! It will cause a draught, mess your hair up and probably give you a blinding headache in the process, but as far as keeping you awake is concerned? I'm afraid not.

What about drinking plenty of water?

Well, if you are going to take the water advice, make sure you get yourself a very large plastic bottle and stick it under your seat, because if you don't, I can assure you you'll be praying to see a 'Take a Break' sign. There is an upside though. Dying to use the toilet will definitely keep you awake. Unfortunately the downside is you do run the risk of wetting yourself in the process.

The thing is, these so called 'experts' are only giving out this kind of advice because it's the healthy option and because it sounds good, but the idea surely is for us to stay awake isn't it? We're not on some sort of healthy regime here; we're trying to stay alive.

Now six Mars Bars and a triple strength Americano coffee on the other hand, they WILL keep you awake.

The trouble is, you will never see either of those put on a motorway sign, or mentioned in the Highway Code book, and the reason for that is they're far too unhealthy. Eating half a dozen Mars Bars and guzzling down a pint of caffeine though, is much better than nodding off at 70 mph isn't it?

I recently travelled down to Tenby in South Wales and needed to head back on the same day (360-mile round trip). 'This is a journey that is definitely going to test out my driving tiredness skills,' I thought. I wasn't disappointed either.

It was very late when I started on my trek back home, but I was okay, everything was fine. I was alert and was feeling quite perky.

Unfortunately it wasn't too long before I started to feel the effects of tiredness, and although Monmouth had seemed a bit blurry around the edges as I passed through, I did manage to hang out until Ross-on-Wye before deciding that it was probably about time I pulled over and got myself my usual fix of coffee and chocolate.

The trouble was, I was now on the M50, and anyone that knows it will know that it's not the most exciting road in the world. In fact it's a complete nightmare for any driver who is tired and is desperately trying to stay awake.

The thing is, being 12 miles from the next service station is bad enough, but I was about to be confronted by the worst possible scenario for any nodding off driver… roadworks!

Now, driving along the M50 trying to stay awake at 70 mph is a challenge in itself, but trying to stay awake at 40 mph on a ten-mile-average speed camera stretch is almost impossible, as your eyes become transfixed by the endless line of road traffic cones. Needless to say, it wasn't too long before I found myself falling into an hypnotic state, as the 12-mile stretch of motorway suddenly seemed like 50.

The annoying thing is, there were no roadworks actually going on. There were no vehicles, diggers, workmen or anything. Just thousands of cones. They were also blocking access to the hard shoulder, which meant I couldn't even pull over on that!

Another annoying thing is that this two-lane motorway was in fact STILL a two-lane motorway, even after being coned off, so why was I being forced to travel at 40 mph?

It was terrible. I felt like a baby that was slowly being rocked off to sleep. Cone after cone after cone… Zzzzzzz.

Suddenly after what seemed like weeks, I spotted a service station in the distance, nestling on the banks of the M5.

Then I passed a sign… 'Tiredness Can Kill, Take a Break' Wow… I'd made it!

GOING FOR A WALK WITH THE DOG

You've just got in from work, you've fetched the oven chips out of the freezer and you see the dog sitting there, with his lead in his mouth, patiently waiting for his daily walk around the block.

You have a glance around, but regrettably it looks like it's your turn again, as everyone else seems to be preoccupied, watching yet another stimulating programme on ITV2 called 'Paris Hilton's Bought a New Handbag'.

You fling the chips and a frozen pizza into the oven and yell the customary line,

"I'm just taking the dog for a walk!" and head off on your travels, with a very excited dog in tow.

The trouble is, when people take their dog for a walk, there never seems to be any communication between them and the dog – there's no bond. It's like putting the dustbin out or scrubbing the carpet, it's just another chore, but it doesn't have to be like that, and life doesn't have to be like that either.

Don't say, "I'm taking the dog for a walk," say, "I'm going for a walk with the dog," and enjoy it.

If you take this attitude in life, then nothing will ever be a chore again.

Washing up is a chore for my wife, she absolutely detests it, and it shows very much in her attitude and approach to this very important task.

Once her mission is complete, it is very hard to understand just how she has managed to get through it without breaking half of it in the process.

Looking like somebody has just emptied the whole contents of the washing-up bowl all over the draining board; you are then faced with the most dangerous task of drying it up.

Undertaking this assignment can be a very treacherous activity and always reminds me of when I was a little boy and used to play KerPlunk, but the washing up version of KerPlunk is a lot more risky.

Firstly you have to study the construction for a while, before attempting your first move, and usually the big question I ask myself is, "Shall I move the bread knife first or do I go for the wine glass?" It's a huge decision, as knives and forks have become tangled in what is nothing more than a web of cutlery mayhem. Wine glasses are dangerously balanced on cups and saucers. A plate is hazardously balancing on a frying pan, which is lodged between an eggcup and a cheese grater.

It is hard to believe just how anybody can wash up in this way, but why does she do it? Well it's quite simple; she just doesn't like doing it, just like people don't like taking the dog for a walk. You see them trudging the streets, dragging the poor canine behind them, in a mad panic, because they don't want to miss *The X Factor*.

Some dog walkers you see wired up to their phone, head bobbing as they listen to one of their favourite bands. This is obviously to make their dog walking experience much more bearable and less monotonous.

Others you will see catching up with emails, text messaging, or just chatting on their phone, completely oblivious to the fact that the dog behind them is hopping along, desperately trying to leave his mark on a passing tree.

To these people, man's best friend has sadly become a chore.

Some poor dogs don't even go out at all.

I know a dog that hasn't left the house since 2003. The only time he gets to see a tree, is if *Country File* is on and even that's not guaranteed. If there's a James Bond film on the other side, then he's had it! His occasional walk along the patio to the shed and back is all that he can hope for I'm afraid.

So get out there folks, walk your dog and enjoy every minute and make it a real special moment.

Have a walk, take a seat, have a chat and by doing that, walking the dog will never be a chore again.

YOU DON'T HAVE TO GROW UP IF YOU DON'T WANT TO

You don't have to 'grow up' just because you're growing up…

The problem is, it is very difficult not to 'grow up' within the system we live in.

Eighteen is the obvious milestone. This is when everyone is told that they are fully 'grown up'.

"You're an adult now," they will be told. "You can buy alcohol." So they do… in very large amounts.

They then go out to celebrate, get drunk and then feel ill for days after.

It's fair to say that many kids are drinking alcohol from a very early age anyway, but that magic milestone of 18, means that they can finally go out and get off their faces legally, because 18 means they are now proper 'grownups'…

Isn't it just great being an adult?

Reaching 18 for the majority of people is a bad time in their lives, because those final few carefree childlike thoughts have been swept away, and a full adult life of work, debt and kennel life have taken over.

It doesn't have to be like that though. As Walt Whitman once said,

"Resist much, obey little". And that certainly rings true as far as becoming an adult is concerned.

Having fun, being yourself and not giving in to the pressures of how the world thinks you should be is the way forward.

You don't have to do what everybody else does. It's good to be you and it doesn't matter about the age, because age doesn't mean anything.

I used to like to read comics when I was a boy. *Cor!!* and *The Beezer* were my favourites.

The thing is, just because I've grown up, it doesn't mean I no longer like them. Sitting down and spending ten minutes in the world of Ivor Lott and Tony Broke, is as much fun now as it was when I was nine years old. It's one of my childhood magical worlds and you don't have to say goodbye to it, just because you reach 18.

Growing up the way this world thinks you should grow up stifles your imagination. It locks it away and makes you believe that it's no longer needed. This results in a boring grown up life, a life where imagination and fun belong in the past and not in the future.

You can reverse these thoughts though and it's never too late to unlock them. Even though you're all 'grown up', you can still move forward with a mindset of carefree, inner-child thoughts, and there's no better time to start it than now.

Get on eBay and find yourself a *Beano*, get a *Dandy Annual* from 1974 and relive the magic. Buy yourself a bag of marbles, fetch out your old train set, write yourself a story or paint yourself a picture. Whatever it is that made you feel so magic as a child, bring it back and live it again.

There is so much more to life than 'growing up' and doing so called 'grownup' things. You can still grow up while reading the *Beano*.

I have bumped into many of my childhood friends over the years and the really sad thing is, nearly all of them HAVE 'grown up'. Work, bills, a bottle of wine a night, *The X Factor* and kennel maintenance, is now all they have. The magic has gone, because they're all kept busy, by simply being 'grown up'.

The thing is, it's all about being in your own world and not bogged down in this one. Lift up your drawbridge and retreat to your own magical place. A place of childhood, when nothing seemed to matter. Those so called 'grown up' things will still be here when you get back.

Just ten minutes with 'Tricky Dicky' or 'Minnie the Minx', will do you the world of good, before having to nip out and post that dreaded water rates cheque, I promise you.

Even if you're a fan of *Postman Pat*. If you like it, then watch it. Don't let the pressures of 'grown up' life make you feel that you shouldn't like it, or make you feel silly in any way.

It doesn't matter if your friend turns up with a four-pack of Carling to watch the rugby either. Telling him that you'd rather watch *Postman Pat* instead will show him how 'grown up' you really are.

SUMMER IS THE WORST TIME OF THE YEAR

It's the 6th of June, I'm sitting at my desk and my feet are on fire... Yes folks, summer has finally arrived here in England...

I'm not geared up for hot summers though. Yes, I like my strawberries and cream and my little bit of sunshine, but when it gets too hot, everything becomes unbearable and when it becomes unbearable, I'm afraid all I want to do is sit around and do nothing. I literally have to be dragged away from my desk fan.

This is something that needed to be done the other day, due to the fact that I had to visit my local town to pay in a cheque at the bank, so reluctantly I ventured out.

When I arrived in the High Street, I was confronted by what can only be described as an array of female all-in wrestlers, all walking about in ridiculously tight-fitting hot pants.

As the saying goes 'If you've got it, then flaunt it', but as most of them hadn't – and that included Big Daddy and Giant Haystacks standing just outside Burger King – then the saying 'If you haven't got it, then for God's sake cover it up' would have been more appropriate.

Another reason why I think summer is the worst time of year is sweat and smell.

Sweaty people tend to go out in their droves in the summer and usually are found lingering around in supermarkets. You can usually detect one by the apparent lack of people around them. People that have unfortunately witnessed the pong at full throttle and have since evacuated to another aisle.

Sweaty men in vests are horrendous, especially when they're reaching up for things, swinging their arms about, or scratching their head because they can't decide on which cereal to go for.

The thing is, if you're going to expose your bare hairy armpits in public, then please have the decency to introduce them to a bar of soap before you go out!

Smelly people can obviously be a problem in the winter too, but, like flies around a turd, it's summer that really brings them out in force.

So what about relaxing in the garden on a beautiful summer's evening? Lovely isn't it?

You're sitting there enjoying a nice cool drink, happy because at last the unbearable heat has died down and you can finally relax in the cool summer's breeze.

You then sit and watch the sun go down, before finally taking yourself off to bed.

What a lovely evening you've had, or so you'd thought.

Reality hits, when you suddenly notice a dozen gnat bites on your right foot... Then the itching starts, the humidity returns and the constant scratching begins.

The problem is that there isn't any barrier against gnats. You could be wearing a set of long johns, six pairs of socks and a frogman's outfit, but a gnat will still somehow find its way in and devour your big toe.

Gnats are just the tip of the iceberg though.

You've got spiders setting up home in your home, when there's a perfectly good shed in the garden. You've got wasps turning up, determined to make your life hell, and you suddenly find yourself having to abandon your long-awaited family picnic as a full-blown attack leads to a complete evacuation of the garden.

Then you've got kamikaze flies whizzing around the house, impossible to catch, as they look around for things to land on and consequently throw up on.

Summer brings noise too, especially if you live on an housing estate.

If you don't believe me, then try and relax in your dog run on a Sunday and you'll soon find that it won't be too long before the lawnmower brigade are out in force, giving that little patch of green that surrounds their treasured kennel the weekly trim.

You will also have to contend with noisy kids, brain-bursting music, dogs barking nonstop (especially if you live in a Jack Russell Zone) and 'Bob the Builder' across the road, who had various noisy tools for Christmas and insists on using them every single weekend.

Even if, by some miracle, you happen to find yourself in a rare moment of silence, I can guarantee that it will be short lived, as someone somewhere will be about to take his hedge trimmer out of the shed to embark on his usual, weekly, hour-long noisy hedge pruning session.

If that isn't bad enough, he will then turn Radio 2 up as loud as he can, because he will no longer be able to hear it over the noise.

Summer is definitely a season to be missed as far as I'm concerned. It's hot, smelly, irritating and noisy and as I'm sitting here listening to yet another lawnmower start up, I'm thinking just one thing… Roll on winter.

WHY WORRY TODAY, WHEN YOU CAN WORRY TOMORROW?

I have always believed that there is no real point in worrying. Obviously if there's an illness in the family, or someone close to you has gone missing, then clearly that's going to give you reason for concern, but for everything else, worry about it tomorrow.

Everyone worries about something, whether it's the mortgage, credit cards, utility bills or whether it's just forgetting to book the car in for a service, but whatever your worry is, just remember that whatever happens, you will always be okay.

Owing money is a major concern for many people, but it's not a crime, you will not be sent to jail for it and it's certainly not the end of the world if you're late with the gas bill.

Have you ever heard of Peter Jarvis?

Well, he was a coal miner. He was born in 1890 and is buried in a cemetery in Northampton. He was troubled all his life and worried about absolutely everything; In fact a day didn't go by without Peter distressing about something or other.

Do you know him? Exactly! This man worried himself sick for 68 years, yet no one today has a clue who he is. It's like he never existed,

"Peter Jarvis? Who the hell's that? Never heard of him!" So what was he worrying about? He might just as well have said,

"Stuff it; I'm going to have a damn good life".

Getting a dog can apparently help us all in the fight against worry. All the experts tell us to do it. They say that owning a dog is the best remedy to keep us all stress free.

The problem with that is, as soon as we've got one, we are then constantly being told to worry about it.

Has it had its inoculations? Is it eating the correct food? Is it getting regular health checks?

This scaremongering is designed to make people fearful, which then makes them rush out to get pet insurance, just in case they need to take out a second mortgage to cover any future vet bills.

When I was a little boy I had two dogs, neither of them had any inoculations, or visited a vet, but both lived until they were 18.

They had exactly the same food as us; they loved crisps and were both partial to a Yorkshire pudding.

Now I know these are not quite the dietary guidelines that are set out by the vet community, but I can honestly say that I don't recall either of them ever hobbling around with arthritis, wearing incontinence pants, or needing a Stannah stairlift to get to bed.

The trouble is, the system we live in encourages us all to worry, because it doesn't want us to do anything else. It doesn't want us to be creative, it doesn't want us to be free, it just wants to dumb us all down and keep everyone in their place.

We are constantly being encouraged to worry, by telling us the consequences of not having things like pet insurance, mortgage protection, house insurance, life insurance, private pension and so on, but at the end of the day, do we really need them?

About ten years ago, I broke down in my car on the M6, but didn't have any roadside cover. This meant that it cost me £100 to get my car towed home. A friend of mine said that if I'd had breakdown cover, then it wouldn't have cost me anything at all and that I would have still had £100 in my pocket.

The thing is, I've been driving now for 37 years and only once have I ever had to call for any assistance.

My friend's breakdown cover on the other hand costs him £60 a year, so I reckon I'm quid's in, as I've only paid £100 in 37.

I can't see the point in worrying about what might happen in the future.

If the boiler breaks down today, then I'll get it fixed. I refuse to get sucked into this paying £12-a-month baloney, on the off-chance that it might pack up next week.

Many people worry about their finances and how they are going to pay their monthly bills.

The biggest cause for worry is direct debits, because they always have to be paid by a certain date and will be taken out, whatever their financial situation is. This can cause unnecessary worry as payments can be returned, and then their bank will charge them interest.

You may be sitting there now worrying sick about a particular direct debit that is due to leave your account on the 15th, but haven't got a clue how it's going to be paid by then.

Well, take the worry away, take control and cancel all direct debits. If a payment is due on the 15th then pay it on the 20th instead. Does it really matter if it's a few days late?

Companies will bend over backwards to entice us into paying by direct debit.

We are made to feel that direct debits are the 'norm' and that there is no other option, but direct debits are just another form of control.

Most people will say that direct debits are wonderful, convenient and just another bill that they don't have to worry about, but in reality they have been sucked into a system and have totally lost control.

I used to pay for my television license by direct debit, but decided to cancel it and pay by cheque instead.

Within a few days I received a letter wanting to know why I had cancelled the arrangement, stating that they wanted to 'help me resolve the situation'. But what situation was they on about? As far as I was concerned, there wasn't one. I was still going to pay, but on my terms and not on theirs.

The real reason is that they know I am no longer in their clutches. I am free and not helplessly manacled to a direct debit system. They don't like the idea that I am on the loose.

The thing is, the more people they get to pay their bills electronically, the sooner cheque books will be phased out and if that happens, it will be a disaster.

Why Worry Today?

What's the point in worrying?
Why live your life in fear
In another hundred years
You won't even be here

Those worries will be long gone
So live your life to the full
Make your life a happy one
Don't live your life dull

Because it really isn't worth it
It will just fill your life with sorrow
So why worry today
When you can worry tomorrow?

CAN I GO BACK IN TIME AND MAKE A NAME FOR MYSELF PLEASE?

Writers from the past used to write essays and meet every day in the taverns.

I get a lovely picture in my head when I think of that. Sounds so much better than writing blogs and boozing down the pub every day doesn't it? Sort of knocks the magic out of it really. But I suppose that's what it was back in the day... Or was it?

Well no it wasn't actually, because back in the days of essays and taverns, writers would head off to London and network within a small community of other writers and publishers. This obviously made it a lot easier for them to make a name for themselves, which is something that you wouldn't be able to do today.

In 1737, Samuel Johnson moved to London Town to do just that, and a name for himself he did make.

Jump forward 280 years though, and the Samuel Johnson of 2017 would find it a hell of a lot harder than he did back then.

Firstly, if he did decide to take himself off to London, then he would have to realise that there are now nine million people living there. That's three million people more than lived in the whole of the UK in 1737.

What about the internet though?

Well, this of course would have benefited Samuel greatly, but the only problem with that is everyone's a writer now and with a blog being set up and posted every half a second, and three million books being published every year, Samuel would very soon find himself returning back home to Lichfield, buried in the writer's jungle, desperately trying to promote himself on Twitter and Facebook, complete with millions of others, all doing exactly the same. Millions of writers right across the world, all claiming to be number-one bestselling authors.

This means that it wouldn't be too long, before Samuel would be taking himself off down the self-publishing route, quickly followed by a 99p Kindle edition on Amazon.

Yes, it's a very different world now to what it was in Samuel Johnson's day.

The trouble is today, there are too many people trying to get through too many closed doors.

But when did they all start closing?

Well, I reckon they started closing about 50 years ago.

Before that, there wasn't really much going on, was there? Not much happening in radio, and TV was only just starting out, so that was relatively easy to get into. In fact you could turn up at the BBC to deliver a parcel and find yourself presenting a new kids programme by the afternoon, it was that easy. These days you need a degree in media studies just to make the tea.

It's probably worth pointing out at this stage that even Steven Spielberg would struggle to get a job now, as he was classed as a 'failure' at school, like so many other creative people are.

Being a success at school and passing exams doesn't mean you actually know anything at all really though. It just means that you've got a good memory. As long as you can remember something that you have been told or read, then you'll be okay (even if you don't understand the answers). In other words, as long as you can remember it, you'll pass it.

The consequence of this of course is a lack of true talent and creativity, leaving the real creative people with far too many walls and obstacles to climb over, in a world that has too many people in it.

True talent and originality doesn't really stand much of a chance does it?

Imagine David Bowie or Morrissey on *The X Factor*? They just wouldn't make the grade, would they?

Morrissey singing 'Dancing Queen' on the ABBA week just wouldn't work.

To be honest, he wouldn't even get past the audition shows. A sarcastic remark off Cowell and a quick embarrassing appearance on *The Xtra Factor* on ITV2 is about as much as he could hope for. Another one left to fend for himself, in the world of social media and self-promotion.

Just like the millions of 'million selling authors', Morrissey is left to fill out his own bio on his Twitter page, just like the millions of other singer songwriters.

'Morrissey, Singer Songwriter, Bit of a Poet, X Factor Contestant, EP now available to download via iTunes, please retweet'

Of course nobody will retweet and nobody will download the EP either (apart from his mum and dad and a few mates from down the pub) but that's the way it is now. I'm afraid the Morrissey of today, would be left scratching his head, trying to work out his next move.

FORCED FUN

I can quite easily give the impression that I am doing nothing. I can stare out of the window for long periods of time and although it may look like I'm doing nothing at all, I am in fact being very creative and doing quite a lot.

Looking at clouds, staring into space or watching the waves splash against the rocks, is all doing something to me.

Your mind and imagination are working overtime, you're producing, you're thinking and you're being creative. Your mind is doing something that most people with a work ethic mentality, just cannot do.

Sometimes if I'm out and I just don't feel like doing anything or talking to anyone, I will just sit and be quiet. You can still have fun while giving the impression of doing very little you know?

Unfortunately this is hard to do, when the forced fun brigade are out, especially at parties.

Here's a perfect example.

You're sitting there being all nice and quiet, sipping your beer and keeping yourself to yourself, when all of a sudden, the conga line turns up, drags you up and then traipses you around the room half a dozen times, to the happy sound of 'Everyone Do the Conga'.

The problem with this is if you don't get up, then people think that you're being rude or a party pooper, but if you don't want to get up, then you don't want to get up!

The trouble is people feel pressurised into doing something by others and they shouldn't. If you feel like doing nothing, then do precisely that... nothing. It doesn't mean you're not enjoying yourself.

In fact, the person sitting around doing nothing is probably having a far much better time than everyone else in there. While he's chilling, people watching, getting ideas and doing exactly what HE wants to do, everyone else around him will mainly be doing exactly what they don't want to do...

Usually you'll find it's forced dancing, followed by a pointless conversation with someone that you haven't seen in over ten years. A person who has taken it upon themselves to tell you all about their neighbours' son, who you have never met before, but now know all the ins and outs of his marriage, his new job and what car he now drives, following a mishap with a tractor last year while on holiday in France.

It's all pointless drivel and it's cluttering up your mind.

As the wittering around you continues, your only hope is that the DJ will put 'YMCA' or 'Dancing Queen' on. At least then you are guaranteed some breathing space, as everyone suddenly rushes to the dancefloor.

Unfortunately your joy is short-lived though, as you suddenly find yourself being dragged up and forced to join in as well.

And this is the big problem with parties...

It's very difficult to enjoy yourself while doing nothing, because there is always somebody there who thinks you should be doing something. There's always somebody trying to spoil your fun.

Only when you are truly alone, can you completely be safe.

Unfortunately this cannot always be possible, particularly if you are in a public place and even though you have put in safeguards, you will find that on the odd occasion, you will be sifted out.

Visiting a town where nobody knows you, is usually a safe option, but this is not guaranteed.

Picture the scene… You've found a nice little pub and you're gazing out of the window, taking in the surroundings.

You're just about to take a sip of your beer, when all of a sudden, you hear the words.

"Stuart! Fancy seeing you in here!"

As you turn, your heart sinks, as you begin to realise the next 30 minutes of your life, will be taken up by talk of holidays in Spain, latest deals from Argos and why their friend in Manchester (who you have never met) is getting divorced for the second time.

As you stare at them, desperately hoping for the conversation to end, all you can think to yourself is,

'Please go away and leave me alone, I'm trying to have some fun… On my own!'

PLAYING-OUT IS THE NEW PLAYING-IN

When I was a kid, we used to play-out on our bikes and kick a ball about, but now you won't see any kids playing-out at all. That's because they're all too busy on their gaming consoles, blowing each other up and playing Pokémon. So instead of playing-OUT with Tommy who lives three doors away, they're now playing-IN with Tommy, who lives three doors away.

I don't see this as a bad thing though.

In my childhood, I had a friend who left the area, because his family wanted to up sticks and go and live in Australia.

It was a terrible time for me, because we were really close friends, but because he'd gone to live on the other side of the world, keeping in touch was difficult and eventually we lost contact.

Now let's fast forward to the Tommy of today who lives three doors away.

If his family decided to go and live in Australia, then nothing would change at all would it? The playing would just continue as normal, so it really doesn't matter anymore if you move away or not. The playing-IN is the new playing-OUT.

My son plays online with his friend, who also happens to live three doors away. They play every day and that's because the new way of playing, allows them to do just that. It doesn't matter if it's raining or snowing or whether it's cold, windy or stormy, it just doesn't matter anymore. Whatever the weather... They play.

Those days have gone, when your mum stands in the street and shouts.

"Come on, it's time to come in now. It's getting dark!" Because getting dark doesn't matter anymore. Playing stays the same.

Going on holiday doesn't matter either.

My son's friend went to Florida for a fortnight last year, but that didn't stop them playing at all.

Following a few hours walk around Disney World, his friend would be back online, playing Mario Kart and carrying on from just where they had left off the day before he went.

It was like he was still three doors away. It was just like he hadn't gone away.

This is the way the world is now, it's all of a sudden become a much smaller place. If you want to go out and play, you just stop in...

You hear a lot of talk from grownups who say that it's not healthy for kids.

They will dwell on the fact that they were always out playing when they were young and that the kids of today need to get out and play properly.

But what you have to remember is, we only had a ball and a bike didn't we?. We didn't have a PS4 or an Xbox! So what you've got to ask yourself is this. What would you have done, if you had opened a PS4 for Christmas in 1974?

And this is the thing isn't it? We can't criticise the kids for playing in this way, because we would have done exactly the same.

Playing-out but playing-in should not be looked at as a bad thing and we shouldn't put a downer on it. We should embrace it, because it's something that benefits all of us, young and old.

I know a little boy who loves playing cards with his Nan, and although he lives 200 miles away from her, it's not a problem, because they can play online anytime. However, if he had been a little boy from years gone by, then he would have had to wait for his six-monthly holiday visit!

Technology of today brings people together, no matter what age, what the time is, or where they live.

All ages can communicate together. They can Skype, message, live chat, join groups, play games, the list is endless.

I know elderly people whose lives have been re-energised by social media, as they have been able to connect with likeminded people, make new friends, and find old ones too.

They are doing exactly what the young ones are being told not to do. They are playing-out, but playing-in, which in my book is wonderful.

So let's not look back. Let's rejoice in our technology, because even though it seemed great kicking a ball about in 1974, you would have given anything to play Maria Kart in 2017, and instead of waking up and losing a friend to the other side of the world, you would have simply just logged on the following morning and carried on playing, where you left off, reaching the next level of Mario Kart together.

ISN'T WINTER WONDERFUL?

Being cold and getting wet is something most people dread, but in fact it can be a wonderful thing. Just embrace it and look for the positives and soon you will realise that winter is such a wonderful time of the year.

Unlike summer, winter is tranquil. You can lock yourself away and sit by the fire, knowing for well, you are not going to be disturbed by some manic neighbour with a lawnmower or hedge trimmer.

It's a time of reflection and contemplation and is a perfect time to shut yourself away from this place they call world.

You can wrap up and go out for a walk in the cold, day or night, wind or rain, it doesn't matter which and it doesn't matter how cold you get, because you know a nice hot bath awaits you when you return home.

This is then followed by a relaxing cosy night in by the fire, feet up, sipping on your favourite drink while wrapped up in a fluffy dressing gown.

This is why winter is so great.

I am currently writing this chapter in July. July is generally a warm, sunny month, but luckily for me, today is wet and windy with a wintery feel to it.

This is perfect, because it's so quiet outside. The hordes of sun worshippers have been defeated and have retreated back into their kennels.

I, on the other hand, am quite content, as I sit here writing with nothing more than a cup of tea, pen and paper and a chorus of birds, all chirping away at me in the beautiful tree, just outside the window.

Winter is also great for sitting in pubs, especially if it's snowing outside.

Sitting in a pub, supping a pint in front of an open fire, is a wonderful way to wind away a couple of hours (on your own obviously)

It's a perfect way to contemplate, people watch and relax.

This is made even better by the fact that outside it's cold, wet and miserable, and even better if it's snowing.

Snow gives people the feeling of being cut off and trapped, unable to escape, but in a good way. It helps people reflect on life. It gives people time to sort things out and find their own little world.

Sometimes people can only do that, if they feel there is nowhere else to go and winter is perfect for helping people realise this.

When you decide to leave your cosy pub and brave the wind, rain, hail or snow, you venture outside and head off home.

It may sound like a journey home that you could well do without, but it's a journey that you should relish. Yes, it may be cold and it may be wet, but enjoy the walk, it's a special moment.

Yes, you've left a warm, cosy environment and ventured off into a cold and possibly freezing one, but don't forget once home, you can take a dip and relax in that nice hot bubbly bath, made even more heavenly by the sound of winter outside.

Sometimes I will go out with very little on, just so that I can feel the benefits of the hot soak when I get back home, but that's just personal preference. You choose the layers.

Another wonderful benefit of winter is to be parked up in your car, on a crisp frosty morning, with the heater on, watching the world go by, as you contentedly sit and relax in yours.

You know it's freezing outside, but you're safe, you're warm, it's your domain and it's special to you.

Yes, winter is a wonderful time and don't let anyone tell you any different. Embrace it, enjoy it, get cosy and run the bath.

Enjoy the isolation, relish the quietness, that quiet at times, it's deafening... Wonderful.

You need to make sure you take it all in though and enjoy as much as winter as you possibly can, because I can guarantee, it won't be too long before the chaos begins and the dreaded hedge trimmers will be back.

IF YOU LIKE DIY SO MUCH, THEN WHY DON'T YOU SMILE?

You look for a house, you get a mortgage, you move in and then you spend the next 25 years doing it up… Why?

Warm, homely and lived in. Those are the only ingredients you need for a happy home.

My wife's side of the family are all DIYers. They live an existence of knocking down walls, altering bathrooms and installing kitchens.

The trouble is, DIYers think that you should be doing exactly the same as they are.

My birthday present off the in-laws a few years ago was a DIY book. At the time I didn't think much of it, but looking back, I now realise that it was not so much as a birthday present, but more of a 'this is what we think you should be doing around the house' type of present.

If that wasn't a big enough hint, they even bought me a workbench for Christmas. Needless to say, the workbench was never assembled and the DIY book went in the bin.

People who spend all their time doing things around the house, are generally unhappy people. They are constantly on the go and always find a need to alter every room in the house.

They also talk as if someone has forced them to do it, but nobody has, it's all self-inflicted.

DIY people are always banging on about what they are doing, what jobs they are planning next and how much they love doing it, but they don't. They can't do, because if they loved it so much, why don't they ever smile?

If you don't believe me, then walk around B&Q on any day of the week and see if you can see anyone in there smiling? You won't see it, because it doesn't happen and the reason why it doesn't happen, is because they are DIYers and being miserable is the norm.

Go and ask any DIYer (if you dare) what their next project is going to be and they will usually sigh, pull a face and then moan on and on about the coming weeks of work that needs to be done. They will always give the impression of doom and gloom, but secretly they like it.

They like the fact that their project will take longer than expected. They like the fact that the previous occupants fitted a twin socket too high up the wall and now it needs to be moved down nearer the skirting. They like the fact that a wall's got to come down, but it can't until the electrics have been moved. They absolutely thrive on it.

Unfortunately it's an illness and all DIYers are exactly the same. They all suffer from the same chronic symptoms and I'm afraid it's a condition that is incurable. To be honest, even if there was a cure, I don't really think they'd want to get better anyway.

DIYers think that being a DIYer makes you a perfect human being and that everyone else will find a DIYer interesting, but they won't and that includes me.

To be honest, I would rather be locked in a room with a guitarist, than have to sit and listen to a DIYer rabble on all night about the next patio that he or she is planning to build.

You will also find that when a DIYer explains anything to you, they will always act as if you should know as well. This is just part of their illness. They don't really expect you to know at all really and even if you do know, they will always know a better way than you do anyway, so it's best to just keep quiet and not say anything at all.

I must point out at this stage, that I am not talking about the *'it's got to be done DIYers'*. DIYers who are forced into small DIY jobs through necessity or wife-nagging circumstances. I am purely talking about hardcore enthusiasts, who live and breathe this ridiculous pastime. I am talking about DIYers who could quite easily restock B&Q, by simply emptying their garage. I'm talking about DIYers who will talk your head off relentlessly for hours and hours, if you dare mention anything remotely connected with DIY.

I made the mistake of saying Rawlplug in a conversation once to somebody and lived to regret it.

It was just the excuse the DIYer needed to spring into action, triggering off a full blown account of how he built his kitchen extension and why he used one inch metal channel instead of 50x50 trunking. Forty-five minutes of my life gone, never to return.

So there you have it!

DIYers are a very strange breed. They're unhappy, they moan, they never smile, BUT secretly love everything about it.

So is there a cure? Well unfortunately not for the DIYer, but there is for you... Avoid them at all costs!

GET IT RIGHT IN THE FIRST PLACE?

They spend £50 million on a new road junction, and then 12 months later the road cones come out, the traffic jams begin and all because someone somewhere, has decided that it now needs a new bollard.

Hang on though! What about widening it a bit and moving the bus stop? That's a good idea isn't it? It'll only cost another million.

But hold up! What about the ridiculously high speed bumps that were implemented just six months before? Never mind… we won't need them now, will we?

Why do things get changed all the time?

Why after careful planning and design, does an original idea get changed and changed and then changed again? It obviously wasn't right in the first place was it?

Many years ago visiting my local town was a pleasant experience. A five mile journey on a single-lane A-road was quite sufficient for the amount of traffic that passed along this particular route every day.

Unfortunately as the years went by and traffic numbers grew, it was decided that a dual carriageway was needed on part of the route, to cope with the demand.

Fair enough, this makes sense. More traffic, so build an extra lane. What a great idea!

Work commenced, and within 12 months a spanking new dual carriageway was in place. Traffic was flowing freely and speed had been increased to 50 mph from 30 mph… Fantastic! All those months of careful planning had finally paid off. We now had the perfect road, or did we?

Well you would have thought so wouldn't you? But no! Apparently not… It was decided that the dual carriageway needed a bus lane, so the dreaded road cones reappeared and another 12 months of road works began.

Let's jump forward to the present day. What do we have now?

What we have now is a dual carriageway with one lane; complete with a 30 mph speed limit… That's exactly the same as it was 35 years ago, except this time there's a constant traffic jam, with thousands of cars, slowly nudging forward, all desperately trying to reach the town centre.

The bus lane meanwhile is completely clear, apart from the odd bus that occasionally whizzes past about every 15 minutes, usually empty may I add, due to the fact that everyone is travelling by car!

Just down the road from this nightmare we have a tram system.

It was built in 1995 at a cost of £145 million…But we had one before… In fact we had them all over the place. You could jump on a tram and travel anywhere across the borough, which begs the question… Why didn't we keep them in the first place?

This amazing network of tramlines were built on practically every street, with the work being carried out over a very short period of time. It was an astonishing feat of engineering.

Now let me tell you about the new tram network.

The new tram network consists of one track... And that's it!

They have now decided after 20 years, that it might be a good idea to have a second track. Unfortunately they can't start yet, because they've got to make the main tram platform bigger, as it wasn't big enough in the first place.

Not getting it right in the first place is everywhere!

Walking around a local shopping centre the other day, I sat on a bench and had a look around.

It was a typical 'We didn't get it right in the first place' kind of a shopping centre and to be honest looking at it, I don't think they ever will.

I remember it starting off life in the early seventies with stairs, two escalators, one lift and a spiral ramp in the middle, but over the years it has had many changes.

One particular time it had three lifts, four escalators (two at one end and two at the other) and a staircase in the middle, where the spiral ramp had once been.

Then we had two bigger lifts, three escalators (two in the middle and one where the other lift used to be) spiral stairs (not ramp) AND straight stairs.

To be honest the straight stairs were useful, as they used to lead you out to other shops that were situated outside. Unfortunately they have now sold this space to New Look, which means the straight stairs don't lead you anywhere now, apart from a window display full of handbags.

I suppose it won't be long before it's all changed again...

I wonder what their next plan will be?

How about something that is simple and cheap? How about something that everyone can use at the same time?

That's it! We need something that is universal for everyone. Able-bodied people, old people, mums with pushchairs and people in wheelchairs.

Yes, I've got it! A spiral ramp…

Maybe it will make a comeback?

I doubt it very much. Ditched over 35 years ago, but something they definitely got right in the first place.

HAVE YOU MARRIED A SNORER?

When you hook up with someone, you really have to seriously consider your future together, especially in the snoring department, because your next 50 or 60 years sleep could depend on how loud and how ferocious your partner's snoring is.

Luckily for me my bride didn't snore, so our marriage was able to go ahead.

The trouble is (to my horror) my wife has started snoring after 30 years of marriage and there's nothing I can do about it either, apart from put up with it, change rooms or get a divorce. I'm not sure which one I'm going for at the moment, but all three are on the table.

So let this be a warning to everyone out there... You just don't know if you're going to end up with a snorer.

To be fair, my wife has tried various techniques to bring her new annoying snoring habit to a halt though, such as nose sticker strips, teeth shields (that keep her mouth open) and nasal sprays, but nothing seems to work.

She's trying another tactic now... It's called blaming me for it.

She's started saying things like

"You must be a very light sleeper," AND "Maybe you don't need so much sleep anymore?" ALSO "Maybe it's because you sit around a lot?" Followed by that classic "If you were out chopping trees down all day, then you probably wouldn't hear me" And only this morning she turned round and said "Well you did go to bed early didn't you?"

Now I don't know about you, but I don't actually class midnight as going to bed early and as it was half past five this morning when she said it, I can certainly tell you one thing, a good night's sleep was definitely not had by me.

Anyway, I decided to get up and put this snoring experience to good use and write this chapter AND yes, I am still tired.

I have also been doing some internet research on the matter and one article I came across said:

'Snoring is very common, with around 40% of the population snoring, but it usually isn't a cause for concern.'

Well it is for me isn't it, because I'm the one that's lying next to one?

These types of stats make me smile to be honest.

How do they know it's 40% anyway? My wife snores, but no one else knows about it but me. Well everyone does now obviously, but you know what I mean don't you?

The thing is, no one has actually turned up at the door with a clipboard under their arm asking her. Even if they had, she could just lie anyway couldn't she? And I bet a lot of people do, or even better, don't even know.

Think about it… If you lived on your own, how the hell would you know if you snored or not anyway? You're asleep aren't you? The only reason my wife knows she snores all night, is because I've told her about it.

The one good thing about my wife's snoring is it's intermittent. It's a bit hit and miss, which means that some nights, I do actually get some sleep.

Usually I know I'm in for a bad night, when she starts snoring before she's even nodded off.

Other nights she will go four or five hours without the slightest hint of a snore, but then she'll suddenly hit me with a couple of grunts, a snort and then a whooshing noise, which is then usually followed by a minute's silence, before hitting me again with any of the above. I call this pot luck night, because I never know what noise I will be kept awake with, or when.

It's also the worst type of snoring, because even the silent bits keep you awake, because you know something is on its way, but you don't know what and you don't know when.

My friend's husband is what I call a predictable snorer. He will snore every night, for six hours at 3000 decibels.

Another friend's husband is also a predictable snorer, but is even louder than that, which means he now sleeps in the garden, with the poor chickens.

The thing is when you marry someone, you vow 'to have and to hold, from this day forward, for better, for worse, for richer, for poorer, in sickness and in health…' But there's no mention of snoring is there? Maybe this should be taken into account when making those wedding vows, because at some point in married life, there's a very good chance that it will rear its ugly head.

Big posh wedding? Expensive honeymoon? Probably best if you invest in a decent sofa as well, because do you know what? You just never know when you may need it.

TAKING MYSELF OFF TO THOUSANDS OF MAGICAL WORLDS

Going off to a magical world is something that many people would love to do.

Well you may be surprised to know that this is possible and is something that I am doing all the time. It's called going to bed, and going to bed to me means that I can go to whatever magical place I want. I simply snuggle down, think of a place and away I go.

Sometimes I might not actually turn up at the place that I was thinking about, but even then it's wonderful, magical and guess what? It's all mine and is totally free.

Going to bed is really great.

One night I woke up at about three in the morning with a line in my head.

I got up and stumbled across to my writing pad and with my eyes half shut, wrote it down.

When I woke up next morning, I went over to see what I had written... It read:

'I believe in freedom, that's how my life is now.'

How brilliant is that?

If I hadn't have written that down, I probably wouldn't have remembered it in the morning.

What's amazing about that is, I didn't puzzle my head trying to think of it. It's not something that I'd sat to contemplate over. I dreamt it with no thought at all, yet somehow the line sums up exactly how my life was then.

I love taking myself off to one of my magical places… I've been to hundreds of worlds over the years and every world I visit, is special to me.

I believe that when we go to sleep, we go to a very special place and even though we're not physically doing anything on the outside, we are in fact in a very creative state of mind on the inside.

You're also recharging your batteries while you're asleep, so you should never feel guilty if you ever fancy a nap. Napping is good, no matter what time of day it is.

I live my life in my world within this world and going to bed is just an extension of that. It's great, because it's a world where nobody else can go but me…

Going To Bed

Up the stairs I go
It's the Land of Nod for me
A magical adventure awaits
And the best of all, it's free

I just pull the covers round my head
Shut my eyes and say
Let's go on a journey
To a place far away

I can go anywhere I like
And very often I do
On an adventure that's all mine
It belongs to me, not to you

I could be on a beach
A beach that nobody knows
Or sitting by a river
Watching, as it gently flows

I could be in a mystical forest
Or looking out at a sea of red
Wherever I am, it doesn't really matter
Cuz I always end up in bed.

HEALTHY FOOD ANYONE?

My wife likes baking things, but she likes to bake in a very healthy way, substituting ingredients for more healthier options.

She does this because she is thinking of my wellbeing. The trouble is, it's sometimes hard to know exactly what you're eating.

She made a cheesecake the other day and to be honest, it was nothing like one! It looked like one, but unfortunately tasted more like a quiche. The base was hard too. This was probably due to the fact that she'd made it with buckwheat flour.

When she found out I liked Madeira cake, her eyes lit up! She rushed off into the kitchen and then reappeared two hours later and presented me with my special treat.

I must admit, it's the first time I'd ever had a Madeira cake with fruit and nuts in before, but at least it was healthy.

And that's the problem, she's always looking at healthy-ing food up.

"I think I'll make a rice pudding," she said once and off she went to concoct her mix of Basmati whole grain rice, coconut milk (even though she knows I don't like coconut) and an array of other healthier rice pudding type ingredients.

She does all this in the faint hope that by some miracle it might turn out like a tin of Ambrosia, but of course it never does.

Don't get me wrong. I am grateful and I really do appreciate what she does, but if I'm expecting a rice pudding, I do like it to vaguely resemble one.

The thing is though, when my wife dishes up something alternative like that; at least it's healthy. She's not trying to hide the fact that it might be full of sugar or artificial sweeteners, or too much salt or full of fat, it is completely healthy. What you see is what you get (sort of). She's not pretending they're healthy, they really are.

This can't be said for the 'Free from Range' at supermarkets. You know the one's I'm on about, free from wheat, gluten and dairy etc.

The trouble is, they're not free from sugar are they and there's enough sugar in a stem ginger biscuit to sink a battleship… Trust me, I've tried one.

I've also tried a 'Free from Range' custard cream and wasn't impressed with that either. It was just like someone had plonked a custard flavoured slice of icing sugar in-between two bits of cardboard and at £1.65 for a pack of eight, that's expensive cardboard.

Some companies try and palm food off as some kind of wonderful alternative to the real thing.

I recently checked out some fishless fish fingers from the local health shop. A wonderful sounding alternative, to any vegetarian that likes fish, but just doesn't like eating fish.

So what was it like?

Well the box looked impressive and the picture on the front had definitely got a Captain Bird's Eye look about it, but once I'd got them home, cooked and on the plate, I soon discovered that fishless fish fingers were definitely that… fishless! In fact the only thing that was remotely fishy about this product, was the picture on the box itself.

Another leading brand have also got an impressive array of boxes, all tempting us with their meat free alternatives. Lamb grills, pork steaks, turkey burgers, chicken fillets and dare I say it… fishless fish fingers. Basically they all taste the same; they're just in different shapes.

So what about readymade meals?

Well, the one thing I can guarantee is the impressive picture on the box will definitely not be what will be waiting for you on the inside. It may look like a vegetable curry on the lid, but once you've burst through the cellophane, you'll soon begin to wonder, just how the hell a cat managed to throw up in your vegetable curry container. Mouth-watering gourmet curry on the outside… Cat puke on the inside (or worse).

You must remember that the picture you are looking at is food that has been cooked by a top chef and then painstakingly set up and photographed by a top marketing company… The dollop of gunk you find inside the box wasn't!

So all in all, I'm much better off with my wife's healthy meals, because although I am being duped to a certain extent, I'm not being duped in the same sort of way.

I'm not purposely being misled. She's just trying to cook certain dishes, but healthily. If she makes parsnip soup, she will not show me a picture of a tin of Heinz before she puts it in my dish and the same goes for her quiche-style buckwheat base cheesecake. She hasn't put it in a 'Taste the Difference' box beforehand.

At the end of the day, we should all eat real food. Food that hasn't been slopped into a box by a machine and food that hasn't been dressed up, making us all believe it's something that it isn't.

Next time you walk round a supermarket, have a look around… real food? You'll be struggling to find any.

Take away the processed foods, snacks and sugar and there won't be much left to buy.

People put the best oil in their car, but many people don't put the best oil in their body and do you know what? That's the most important engine of all.

IT'S NOT FOOD, IT'S POLYFILLA

I got up this morning to discover that my wife is now thinking about dishing up rice breakfasts.

This is obviously another one of her healthy ideas that she will no doubt be putting into practice in the near future.

These ideas usually last for about two weeks, until she suddenly discovers something else that she thinks is even more healthy for us.

Porridge is usually the favoured breakfast for my wife though and it's never usually too long before its back on the breakfast menu.

Porridge is something that I'm not a big fan of and although she knows this, she still continues to ask me every morning if I want some.

For generations we have been told that porridge is good for us. It's high in fibre, it reduces blood pressure, it lowers cholesterol, it prevents heart disease and our body just can't get enough of it.

My body struggles with porridge though and to be honest, I'm not really surprised.

To me porridge is like Polyfilla and if you don't believe me, then you try and clean your saucepan after cooking it and tell me I'm wrong? You'll find that the only bit you're not scrubbing is the bit you've just eaten.

Imagine that trying to fight its way around your digestive system. At least you can use a scourer on a saucepan. You can't on your digestive tracts, stomach and colon can you? You just have to let your body get on with it.

When I was a kid I used to collect football cards and always had trouble sticking them in the album. I was constantly running out of glue and so would try and make my own with flour and water.

If only I knew then, what I know now... I would have just simply got my mum to rustle me up a bowl of porridge. In fact I probably wouldn't have even bothered with the glue at all, if I'd have realised at the time just how good porridge was.

There's no doubt about it, porridge was definitely the 1970s version of super glue.

To me it stands to reason that anything that sticks to the pan like concrete, should be avoided at all costs.

Why make your body work overtime, trying to digest something that was obviously intended to fill in cracks? As far as I'm concerned, porridge should be found on the shelves of B&Q next to the tubs of No Nails and not in aisle seven next to the cornflakes.

Washing a porridge saucepan up, as I've mentioned, is a bit of a nightmare, but if you think that's bad enough, you should try washing one up when it's been left overnight. Make this mistake and you'll soon start to wonder if a three-pack of scourers will actually be enough.

So what's the answer?

Well the easiest answer as far as I can see, is to throw the saucepan away, invest in a new one and never eat porridge again, but as my wife loves porridge so much, I'm afraid that's never going to happen.

So what about scrambled eggs?

Well, I think scrambled eggs fall into the same category. They're definitely up there in the Polyfilla stakes anyway. In fact if scrambled eggs (along with porridge) were suddenly made illegal, I am sure every scouring company in the land, would suddenly go out of business.

You leave an unwashed scrambled eggs pan and you will live to regret it. Just ten minutes is enough time for it to harden up... Even Polyfilla takes two hours to go off! Makes you think doesn't it?

Porridge and scrambled eggs?

Don't eat either of them... Just think. If they're doing that to your pans, then they must be playing havoc with your guts.

DON'T LISTEN, CHOCOLATE IS SMALLER

"Chocolate looked bigger then, because you were smaller."

That's usually what people say, if you dare question the size of a Wagon Wheel or a Curly Wurly, but the truth of the matter is, they were definitely bigger than they are today.

Wagon Wheels were originally called Wagon Wheels because they were big, round and did actually resemble one, but I'm afraid the twenty-first century version looks more like a wheel that's dropped off the back of a Barbie dolls shopping trolley.

Curly Wurlys are the same! One alone used to keep my jaws active for most of the day, but now they are so puny, it's hardly worth bothering to clean your teeth afterwards.

The list is endless… Walnut Whips, Smarties, Mars Bars, Topics, Toffee Crisps and Yorkie Bars to name just a few.

The truth is chocolate looked bigger then, because it was!

Do you remember when Yorkie Bars first hit the shelves? They were marketed as this huge chocolate bar feast, that would keep a lorry driver going for days.

He could drive down to Dover, cross the channel, drive down to the South of France and still have four squares left for his trip home.

The lorry driver of today I'm afraid wouldn't even have time to jump in his cab and start the engine, before he'd consumed his Yorkie Bar. In fact he'd probably have to take half a dozen Wagon Wheels with him, just to keep him going.

I get very sceptical when a chocolate bar gets a makeover or a bigger bar is introduced.

A bigger bar usually means you handing over more cash, which is fair enough if your favourite bar of chocolate is going to stay the same size, but it doesn't. Unfortunately it will in time acquire the dreaded confectionery shrinking disease and end up the same size as the smaller bar was, which has since been discontinued. You can guarantee the one thing that won't shrink though, will be the price. That will continue to rise, as your chocolate bar continues to shrink.

Don't be taken in by the marketing people either. They will have you believe that a bar of chocolate will transport you to some heavenly dream world, when the reality is that too much of it will probably send you to the nearest coronary heart unit.

My earliest recollection of chocolate bar marketing goes back to when I was a kid.

The commercial would show a young slim glamour model, on a boat, floating down the river on a beautiful summer's day, hand in the water, pouting her lips, delicately eating her silky-smooth chocolate bar.

I could never really see how a beautiful young girl managed to look like this though, especially after eating a 2 lb slab of chocolate. In the real world, any teenager who ate this amount of chocolate, would very soon end up with a face full of erupting acne. Most teenagers I knew got spots by just sniffing a Cadbury's Cream Egg, so god knows what a 2 lb block of chocolate would do.

Even today the marketing people cannot resist showing us a beautiful young woman, rolling around on a Caribbean beach, caressing a Bounty Bar or a Cadbury's Twirl, when the truth is, it's more likely to be a 22-stone roly poly, planted on a sofa, watching *The X Factor*, while chewing on a king sized Mars Bar.

Yesterday I saw some glamour puss on a poster. She was lying flat out on a sun lounger, somewhere in the South of France. She was smiling at some bronzed hunk and was just about to bite into a bar of chocolate fudge.

The bronzed hunk was enjoying a bar too and was smiling back at her. It was a poster full of teeth! They were perfectly white and not a filling anywhere. It was more like a Colgate toothpaste advertisement.

Next to it was another poster, complete with yet another glamour model in a bikini, binging on what is described in the ad as 'the light way to enjoy chocolate…' The chocolate was at least half the size it was in 1978.

'The most truthful slogan yet,' I thought.

MAKING THE MOST OUT OF YOUR COUNCIL TAX

Paying council tax is a real bugbear of mine, because I can't really see what I'm getting out of it, apart from having my dustbin emptied every Thursday morning and even then they leave most of the rubbish scattered across the road.

This is why when I pay council tax, I milk the occasion as much as I can.

Most people either pay online or by direct debit, but what's the point in that?

The way I see it is… If you're going to be fleeced by your local council, then you might as well make the most of what the council have on offer and that's exactly what I do.

Once a month, I take a trip to my local council offices, intent on handing over my monthly cheque, but at the same time utilising the facilities around me for at least 30 minutes, sometimes an hour before I go home.

Guess what? I am currently writing this chapter, in the council offices on some very nice comfy seats, relaxing with my feet up.

The seats are situated within a lovely carpeted area. I have a table to do my writing on and there's a heater right next to me, which is very nice because it's pretty cold outside.

I very often sit here following the handing over of my monthly dustbin cheque. It's a perfect place to reflect on life and then write about it.

There's even a free drinks machine opposite, just in case I fancy a tea or a coffee, which is very handy, especially if I've been here a while.

Making use of the facilities is a must as far as I'm concerned, as I feel it is very important to make the most out of the money, that the council have siphoned from me.

I always go to the toilet as well (even if I don't need to go) simply because the soap smells nice and it would be a real shame not to use it.

Trying to get as much satisfaction as possible out of my local council offices is very important to me, because as I say, they only empty my bin.

So what about the schools?

Well, as both my kids were home-schooled anyway, all I can see that I've done, is pay for somebody else's. If anything I should have had a refund, but have I…? No!

The same applies to people who don't have any kids. Why should they pay for somebody else's?

What about the local swimming baths?

Well as I can't swim, that doesn't apply to me either, so once again, I am paying for something else that I don't use.

What about the two remaining local libraries?

Well, I tend not to use either of them, as I don't have that much interest in 'Katie Price' or 'Cheryl' and I certainly don't want to know the life story of Harry Styles or read about Olly Murs' Dad.

To be honest, I would rather read a Mark Twain or Jerome K Jerome book, but as both Mark and Jerome have never appeared on *The X Factor* or *I'm a Celebrity Get Me Out of Here*, then I might as well stay at home and order them off Amazon.

So what else am I paying towards?

Well, apparently I'm paying towards council-run car parks.

Unfortunately, this does not mean I can park on council-run car parks for free though! Oh no. I still have to pay £3 a day to park on them, even though I've already paid…

Typical, the only thing I actually do use and here I am, paying for it… Again!

In reality, the only thing that I do benefit from with regards to the Council Tax, is they empty my bin… and that's about it.

I must point out that while I have been writing this book, the council have notified me that due to cut backs, they will now be emptying my dustbin once a fortnight, instead of once weekly…

I wonder if a 50% Council Tax reduction is too much to ask for?

TECHNOLOGY IN THE WRONG HANDS

Technology in the wrong hands can be catastrophic. Hackers can break into government computers, data can be wiped or even stolen and viruses can be sent around the world, causing havoc on PCs everywhere.

But there is something that is much worse and far more worrying than that and that is a 75 year old trying to use a computer!

Hearing those fatal words

"What does this button do?" is usually an indication that they are about to accidently delete over a thousand photographs. These will be the same thousand photographs that you put on for them, just the week before.

It is also an indication that they are about to click on something that is completely pointless and although you have told them at least half a dozen times before that clicking it will not do anything, they will continue to ask and they will continue to click.

So here's my advice.

If you do have any older relatives that are considering buying a new computer, then change your telephone number as quickly as possible, because if you don't, I can assure you, it won't be too long before your telephone number will be used as their personal PC Helpline.

This means you will find yourself on call 24-hours a day, talking them through simple operations, such as creating a new file, saving a document, or even explaining how to switch the damn thing on.

These are of course very simple tasks to the majority of us, but to an elderly person it will feel more like learning to fly Concorde, even though they're only trying to drop three jpegs into their holiday folder.

Also for some reason, elderly people tend to forget usernames and passwords. This leads to many problems, including elderly Apple users constantly being locked out of their accounts.

The problem is, they tend to think that a username and password will never be needed again, but of course they will. So when a reset password is required (because they've been locked out) new problems occur, because the email that they originally used to set the account up with in the first place, cannot be accessed, because they've forgotten that password as well.

The mother-in-law got locked out of her Apple account a few weeks ago, because of this very reason. She just couldn't remember her password at all and she hadn't written it down anywhere either, but why?

Why is it that where technology is concerned, the elderly all go to pot?

They can tell you the day and time the green bin is going to be emptied and they can tell you when the brown bin is going to be emptied. They can also tell you when 'Clean a Bin' are coming to clean the black bin, but you ask them to remember the name of their first pet, so that they can access hundreds of very important personal files and they will stare back at you, with that usual blank look on their face.

This will then follow with 30 minutes of fumbling through old envelopes, in the desperate hope that at some point in their lives, they may have actually written something down somewhere.

"Is it umberella432?" Will come a voice from behind a mountain of envelopes.

It's a clutch at straws really, but it's worth a try, as it's the only password the mother-in-law has got.

Following a few failed attempts in lower case, upper case and a mixture of both, it suddenly dawns on her that 'umberella432' was in fact the answer to the holiday competition on *Loose Women* from six months ago.

Unfortunately this inability to understand technology doesn't stop at computers. It has infiltrated almost everything in life and the elderly just cannot deal with it.

Watching and recording television programmes has come on leaps and bounds over the last 20 years or so, as we have slowly moved into the digital age. This of course has been wonderful for the majority of us, but for the older generation it has been a complete nightmare. Bear in mind that it took most of them ten years to learn how to record *Coronation Street* on a VHS recorder, so what hope in hells chance have they got with a Sky+ box?

So here's some advice.

Whatever technology your old age relative has decided to partake in, whether it be a computer, iPad, Sky+ Box, Smart TV etc… The same guidance always applies… Change your telephone number as soon as possible!

GET RID OF CLUTTER, SORT OUT YOUR BREAD BIN

I love having a good tidy up, especially when the wife has gone out. Everything in the kitchen gets put where it's supposed to be put and it's all done in a nice, relaxed, organised way, over a nice cup of tea.

The only trouble is, she comes back again and within 24 hours, I can guarantee the prunes will be back in the bread bin, the nuts will be in the biscuit tin and the jar of almond butter will be lost forever, never to be seen again.

Now let me tell you about our bread bin.

Our bread bin is extremely difficult to get to, mainly because of the assortment of objects that my wife has decided to place in front of it.

If by any chance I am lucky enough to find bread in there, I then have to decide whether it's really worth trying to fight my way through another obstacle course, to a toaster that is tucked away in the corner, heavily camouflaged, by two bottles of olive oil, a kitchen towel holder, a Nutri-bullet, six kitchen knives, three sieves, a colander, half a dozen wooden spoons and a tin of organic Christmas drinking chocolate? I daren't move the toaster either, because I know within time, it will only manoeuvre itself back to the corner and reposition itself behind all the clutter.

I have really tried my hardest to rectify my wife's inability to be organised and tidy, but unfortunately, it's a losing battle, as she seems to be more interested in making a mess.

So what about the cupboards?

Well, keeping a cupboard tidy is essential as far as I'm concerned, tins together, jars together, spices together etc., but for some reason my wife cannot adapt to this kind of system. She would rather pile everything up, just like she does with the washing up. It's back to the KerPlunk mentality again I'm afraid.

The main problem with this, apart from running the risk of being hit on the head by a jar of pickled onions, is not actually knowing what is in there.

Only last week we bought a bottle of tomato sauce, only to find another two bottles lingering behind the cornflakes when we got home. That's £6.90 in sauce just sitting there, waiting to be used.

So what have my cupboards got to do with you, you may think? Well nothing as it happens, but your cupboards have.

At the end of the day, I'm just pointing out how cluttered our lives can be.

The thing is, it may just seem like a cupboard full of random food objects to you, but it's a cluttered cupboard and a cluttered cupboard is a good indication that your life, is probably very much in the same sort of state.

If this sounds like you, then the time has come for you to clear them out and start again. Line up the tins, sort out the jars, uniform the spices and most importantly… Put the porridge in the shed!

Your cupboards should be able to breathe.

You should be able to open the cupboard doors and see exactly what's in there, without having to juggle with two tins of beans and a bottle of salad cream, while you struggle to find the peanut butter.

Only once you master the art of organising your food cupboard, can you realistically move on and start organising and decluttering the rest of your life.

Don't fall into the trap of buying clutter free accessories either, because clutter free accessories are nothing more than clutter accessories.

They are meant to help you get organied, but in reality, they just end up causing you more work and just generate more clutter.

Don't put shelves up either, because shelves are clutter magnets for people who are vulnerable.

Plastic containers (clutter boxes) or gadgets designed for storing things are also a no no.

This is because:

1) You will not store what you are supposed to store in them, and
2) They will just take up space, adding to the clutter that you already have.

You should also steer away from pedal bins. Not only will they be in the way, but they will also take up valuable space. You will also have the constant chore of cleaning the thing out every few days as well…

So let's recap.

Sort out the cupboards, throw anything out that you don't need, give yourself lots of space and don't buy any 'clutter free' gadgets.

Oh and the most important thing of all…
Make sure your bread bin's just got bread in it…

WHAT IS IT WITH SIGNS?

I admit that some signs can be useful, but for most of them, they are completely pointless and have no use what so ever…

'Baby on Board'… So what?

I very often take my wife out in the car, but I don't put a sign up telling everyone about it.

Me knowing that you've got a baby on board doesn't make me drive any different… I still drive exactly the same.

What about 'Beware of the Dog' and 'Dog Running Freely'? Can someone please tell me how that information is going to help me? I know there's a dog there, because there's a sign telling me about it, but where is it and what can I do to avoid it? I don't know do I, because that vital piece of information is missing!

If I'm delivering a parcel, I've still got to deliver it, dog or no dog, so don't you think it would be a good idea to let me know exactly where the thing is? It would certainly save me getting my legged gnawed off wouldn't it?

Another one is 'Beware of Black Labrador'.

Why black? Are black ones more dangerous than other colours then? What about white ones? What's so special about black Labradors that make them more dangerous, than any other coloured variety?

Then you've got 'I like Poodles', 'I like Cocker spaniels', 'I like Yorkshire Terriers', 'I like Greyhounds' the list is endless. Well do you know something? I like cheese and potato pie and I love mushrooms on toast, but I've never felt the urge to go and put a sign up in my front window about them.

The truth is nobody really cares that you've got a dog, or what breed it is, just like nobody cares about my fetish for cheese and potato pie, so please can you just keep it to yourself?

Then you've got obvious signs. These types of signs are everywhere. You just can't get away from them and they come in all types of guises.

The other day I went out and bought myself a packet of nuts and on the back of the packet was a warning that said 'May Contain Nuts'.

I was really pleased about that, because do you know what? That's exactly what I wanted.

I then glanced up and saw a sign on the wall that was warning me that if the building was to catch fire, then I should evacuate immediately and under no circumstances re-enter it.

I presume that the reason for this is that if I did, then I would probably burn to a cinder and never come out again.

Isn't all this just a little bit obvious though?

The thing is, if I did have a nut allergy, then the last thing I would do, is rush off and buy myself a 500 g packet of salted peanuts and I would certainly not dive back into a building that was engulfed in fire. It's just all common sense isn't it? Or doesn't anyone want us to have any anymore?

I was at a train station the other week and as I left the platform, there was an enormous sign informing me of the way out. The sign was absolutely colossal and was situated above some HUGE double doors. They were wide open to reveal the city centre and as this was the only way out, I thought it was probably a pretty good place to put the sign.

Once outside I spotted a bus station, with a bus station sign above it. I felt that it really didn't need the sign though, as there were about 60 buses all parked up, which was a bit of a giveaway really.

Another sign saying 'Taxis' was pointing towards a taxi rank, with about twenty taxis all lined up waiting for potential customers.

As I headed off towards the city centre, I noticed a sign with... Guess what? You've got it 'City Centre' written on it. I did decide to follow it though, as the only other possible option was for me to jump over a wall and fall 150 feet onto a railway line.

It doesn't matter where you go. There always seems to be a sign that is stating the obvious.

I decided to park my car at a good old-fashioned car park the other day, where a real human being greets you (in my case, Old Fred) and where silly signs do not exist.

Unfortunately this was no longer the case and on my arrival, to my dismay, discovered that Old Fred had gone. The place had been transformed into an NCP car park and instead of a friendly face; I was now greeted by a machine and a churned out ticket.

'Please Take Care of Your Ticket' was the first piece of information that was fed to me.

'Please Don't Lose Your Ticket' was displayed across the wall in front of me.

'Have You Got Your Ticket?' was written directly above the ticket machine.

It made me wonder just how valuable this ticket was! I was half expecting Willy Wonka to jump out and whisk me off somewhere.

When I finally returned from my fifty minute shop, a 'Pay Here' sign greeted me as I entered the car park.

The friendly face of Old Fred had gone and all was left was a machine, along with a 150% price increase.

I inserted my ticket, I paid the money and the ticket came back.

As I glanced up, the message on the display read 'Please Remove Your Ticket and Drive to the Exit'…… Aargghh!!

IN BED WITH MY WIFE

Being in bed with my wife can be very stressful at times (and I'm not just on about the snoring) to a point where I am seriously thinking about getting a new one (bed that is, not wife)

Firstly for some strange reason, she is always hungry as soon as she gets in. She's fine on her way upstairs, but as soon as she gets in bed, she suddenly gets the urge to go straight back down again and fetch herself either an apple, a stick of celery, a carrot, or a plate of crackers... Basically anything that's loud!

She's also got a fascination with angel cards and very often fetches them out, to see who her guardian angel will be for the following week.

This means that getting to sleep can be very difficult, as she is constantly shuffling. Some nights the shuffling is that bad, it's like being in bed with Paul Daniels.

Sometimes I will hang on a while before I get in, usually about 30 minutes. This then gives her plenty enough time to settle in, fetch food, shuffle her cards and work out her numerology numbers etc.

I do have to be very careful I don't leave it too long though, as I then run the risk of her accidently nodding off, which then means an early snoring session is very much a possibility. This will inevitably result in me heading off downstairs and then spending the rest of the night on the sofa.

Sometimes she will be completely oblivious to the fact that I am actually in bed, as all the lights will go on and she will stomp about, chewing very loudly on a large piece of celery.

This is very frustrating for me and something I find quite irritating, because if ever she's in bed before me, I make sure things are very different.

I will plan my route to bed meticulously well, with minimum disturbance to my wife.

I will head upstairs (quietly and in the dark) open the bathroom door, then shut it again BEFORE switching the bathroom light on. Whereas my wife will do the complete opposite!

She will head upstairs (very loudly) eating something extremely crunchy, with ALL the lights on.

She will then open the bedroom door, switch the light on and then take herself off to the bathroom, where she will switch the bathroom light on, with the bathroom door wide open too.

That is how it stays until she finally decides to get back into bed to finish off her nightly snack, have a quick shuffle and then a final trip to the bathroom to clean her teeth, before getting back into bed again.

This is not a delicate operation either, as she tends to jump in at full pelt, sending me a good six inches up into the air.

By this time I am wide awake, which will result in me heading off back downstairs for a cup of tea and an inevitable night on the sofa again.

I am obviously painting quite a negative picture here, highlighting my wife's bedroom antics at their very worse. So I'd just like to point out that occasionally, I do get a night off from these annoying, irritating escapades… Yes, sometimes she will just get in and snore!…

And that's the problem. She's very unpredictable

To me, going to bed should be a very special moment. It's a time when you should be able to fully relax and prepare to take yourself off to one of your magical worlds. You should be able to do this in a calm and relaxed way and not have to worry about trying to get in there and get to sleep before Barry Chuckle turns up.

Unfortunately though, like her washing up and food cupboard organisation skills, I fear that this kind of bed behaviour, will be with us for life, which means regular trips to the sofa, look well and truly on the cards for me.

"Why don't you move and get a bigger house?" people have said.

This of course is a terrific idea and something that I am looking at very closely at the moment. Well it does make a lot of sense doesn't it?

Do you know what? I might even let her visit me sometimes.

AMBUSHED BY THE DOGS TRUST MOB

Nipping out to buy a loaf of bread from Sainsbury's might sound straight forward enough to most people, but it's not as easy as you may think.

Firstly you've got to get from your car to inside the store, without being stopped by anyone on your way in.

This is not as easy as it sounds.

Usually you are confronted by a very friendly RAC man standing by the main entrance, frantically waving a piece of paper in the air, desperately trying to get you to sign up to a 12-month roadside cover policy.

Getting past this very annoying, but very enthusiastic man can be a delicate operation, but with a little bit of planning, it can be achieved.

The first thing you must remember is to never make eye contact, because making eye contact will totally give him the wrong impression. He may actually think that you're interested in buying his product!

If you need some guidance, then here's what you need to do…

As you approach the store, look straight ahead, but whatever you do, don't allow your eyes to stray. As far as you're concerned, the RAC man is invisible… He doesn't exist. You will hear a cry on your approach and as you pass, but you must remember to carry on regardless. Whatever you do, don't stop!

The trouble is, Once past the RAC man, the chances are, you will be accosted by someone else, just inside the entrance, wearing a bright orange jacket, all ready to flog you Sainsbury's Energy.

"Are you interested in earning an extra thousand Nectar points, sir?" you will hear as you enter the store. "You can earn further points if you agree to pay by direct debit, sir" they will shout as they try to block off your only route to the fruit and veg. "Can I ask you who you're with at the moment, sir?" they will say, as they reach for a form.

At this point it's always worth bearing in mind that it doesn't really matter what company you tell them, because Sainsbury's Energy will always be the better deal, even if the current company they are in partnership with, were apparently the worse one when you visited the store a few months earlier.

It is also worth bearing in mind that a thousand Nectar points will only buy you two loaves of bread and a tub of Clover, so it's not really worth getting that excited about.

Walking the streets can also be very treacherous too.

The High Street is very often littered with various charities and organisations, all trying to persuade you to part with £3 a month to help with their cause.

The other week I visited my local town to pick up some rice flour from the health food shop for my wife and nearly ended up adopting a tiger from Siberia in the process. I'd only stopped for a few seconds to check a text message, a decision that almost proved fatal. Luckily I averted my eyes, changed direction and managed to escape.

My joy was short-lived though, because as soon as I'd turned the next corner, I was then set upon by two manic teenagers from the Dogs' Trust.

The thing is when I go out; I just want to go about my business. I don't want to be ambushed on every street corner, by gangs of youths in brightly coloured t-shirts with false smiles and clipboards. I just want to be left alone.

The TV is littered with charity adverts too, all aiming to tap into your bank account on a monthly basis. One charity have gone one even better now though. Forget about the £3 a month direct debit; this charity also want your money when you're dead.

Yes! Even when you've kicked the bucket they're after it.

Have you seen the commercial?

It shows a depressed looking elderly man, writing out his will. He's already decided that he's going to leave his car to his brother Cyril and the house to his wife, but now there's a charity turned up and they want a piece of the action too.

He's just about to sign, when all of a sudden a voice says,

"Do you know that you can now leave part of your estate to us?" He stops to think. "Just 1% will make a difference" the voice spurts.

The commercial ends with us not actually knowing this poor man's final decision, but I can just imagine his poor wife looking on in horror, in the realisation that she could soon just end up with a few quid, if this charity have their way. On the plus side though, at least his brother Cyril's guaranteed the car.

Even sitting in your own home though with your television switched off you're not safe.

A friend came round for a meal a few weeks ago and one of the first things out of his mouth was.

"I'm doing a charity walk next month; do you want to sponsor me?"

Now I don't know if you've ever noticed, but sponsored events are ALWAYS completed successfully. People never fail do they? Even if they are doing a sponsored bungee jump on the moon, complete with an elephant strapped to their back, you will find that they will always return in a few weeks' time, complete with begging bowl, looking for payment.

Realising the fact that this would be the case, I decided to reach into my pocket and fetch him out some money. Yes, I'd decided to bite the bullet and sponsor him…

Well, what's 20p?

WHAT'S THE BIG FASCINATION WITH CELEBRITIES?

A week doesn't seem to go by without some kind of *X Factor* style show hitting our screens.

Teenagers sing their little hearts out, claiming to be on an amazing journey. It's their dream, it means the world to them and of course, they've been waiting for this moment all their life.

But wait a minute, it probably hasn't been that long ago since they were wolfing down alphabet spaghetti on toast, before having to rush out to do a paper round, but now all of a sudden, their life is complete, at the ripe old age of 18.

Everyone loves a celebrity, even when they have only been around for five minutes. Nobody wants to know you one minute, but stand on Katie Price's foot, or marry a footballer and you'll soon find yourself on the front cover of every magazine going.

I always remember when Wayne Rooney broke his fifth metatarsal bone in his foot. He couldn't play football for weeks and the media frenzy that followed was unbelievable. You just couldn't get away from Wayne's foot, as every news item included an update on it.

'What would he do if he was unable to play football again?' That was the question posed by every news source.

My heart used to bleed for this multi-multimillionaire, who could suddenly find himself out of work.

There was no need to worry though, because Wayne was taken straight to hospital, treated and fitted with a state of the art air boot...

When I broke my fifth metatarsal a few years ago, it was a completely different story.

I had to drive 140 miles, wait 48 hours to see a specialist and then once plastered, was offered a blue flip flop to hobble around on.

At the end of the day, I can understand Wayne having the best treatment. He's got the money hasn't he and if you've got the money, that's what you do, but to be bombarded with endless news updates on it, is something that we can all well do without.

The thing is, why does there always have to be a big song and dance, whenever something happens to a celeb?

It doesn't matter how trivial it is either.

Taylor Swift hit the headlines today, because her 15-month romance was over...

So what? It's not exactly a 30-year marriage is it? I've had a Sky TV contract last longer than that!

Last week there was a cracking headline in one of the national newspapers.

'Judy Finnegan enjoys a fun day out with Richard Madeley as they visit a London pub.'

That's nothing though. The week before it was revealed that 'Mel B of Spice Girls fame, unfollowed Mel C on Twitter' and if that wasn't bad enough, she then went and unfollowed her on Instagram!

The alarming thing is, most of the population find this type of news reporting interesting! For many people, it's all they want to talk about! Forget about the important issues that are going on around the world, like wars, poverty and terrorism, as long as they are kept up to date with the latest celeb news, that's all that matters.

By the way, Danielle Lloyd didn't put any makeup on yesterday.

SCHOOL IS BAD FOR YOUR EDUCATION

Not only are kids too young to go to school, but they are also programmed to be identical while they are in there.

Writing is a typical example of this. They are told to write neatly and keep stopping to analyse their work, but surely that is just stopping the child's creative flow?

Most great writers don't work like this. They will just let their ideas pour out onto a piece of paper. The neatness doesn't matter does it? It's the idea and the story that counts.

When I was at school, I wasn't interested in hardly anything, with history being one of my hate subjects. I really couldn't stand it.

My interest has grown over the years though, and today I am really fascinated by it. Basically I was just too young to appreciate it at the time.

Kids are simply too young to go to school. School is a time when they should be out playing and creating. They should be enjoying themselves and not cooped up for all those years. Years of conformity and imprisonment, from nursery and school, right through to college and university.

In between all that of course, they've got breakfast clubs, afternoon clubs and everything else that goes with them. It's a life of constant education. A populace of kids, all being groomed for a system that is waiting for them on the outside.

Isn't it strange how animals don't need any of this?

Birds don't have to send their young to school do they? They know distinctly how to grow up, leave the nest and then go out and look after their own. The parents don't need to say.

"Come on you, isn't it about time you left the nest and got yourself a job?" They just leave and get on with it don't they…? Automatically.

Humans are trapped though. Trapped in a world where everything is planned out for them. It's a world of control with a follow the leader mentality that begins at school.

Both our kids were home-schooled. This has meant that they have had the freedom to do exactly what they have wanted, without the added pressure of having to do things, that they haven't wanted.

Their heads haven't been stifled or suffocated by an education system. An education system that would have just blocked off their creative field and shut them out from their own special world.

By being home-schooled, they have been allowed to be themselves, unlike many children, who are forced to partake in a process, designed to lead them into the prison of life.

Kids should be socialising with people of all ages, doing lots of different things, every day of their lives.

Let their minds wander, let them create and if they want to scribble, then let them scribble!

The world is your classroom. Go out and find it.

It's Your Classroom

You'll sit in a classroom
And then you'll take a test
But why should you toe the line?
And toil like the rest

It's your classroom that counts
Away from all the fools
You can do what you want
Because you set the rules

You can get up at nine
You can get up at ten
You can get up whenever you like to be honest
Because it's you that decides when

You can take a stroll along the river
You can go for a boat ride, that's fun
You can write yourself a story if you want
Or you can just lie about in the sun

Whatever you do just remember
That while everyone else is behind closed doors
Yours will be wide open
Because it's your classroom, all yours

SHALL WE ALL GET DRESSED UP AND PRETEND?

I am currently writing this chapter dressed up as a 1950s doctor.

I've got a suit on complete with waistcoat, jacket, a white doctor's coat AND it's the hottest day of the year, so today should be very interesting to say the least. Luckily I've found a nice spot upstairs on the dining bus, next to the air conditioning fan. Fortunately for me, no one has twigged this yet, which means I've got this refreshing waft all to myself.

I'm working (if you can call it that) on a show where I am playing one of those characters that hardly ever gets seen and even when they are seen, it's usually just a leg, arm, or sometimes nothing at all. Yes, I'm working today as what's known as a supporting artist!

Now I don't know about you, but I can never watch a period drama without thinking how staged it all looks. To me it's like a load of people just playing dress up.

Everything is just too perfect too. Too perfect to be real. For instance…

I've just been in to makeup and had my hair cut, greased and sprayed. There's not a single hair out of place. When

I get on set, I will be checked and probably sprayed again, before they shoot the scene.

The costume department will then make sure my buttons are all done up. They will make sure my tie is perfectly straight and that my 1950s style spectacles, are strategically placed on the end of my nose... but why? Didn't people just get up and get dressed like we do now? I'm sure they didn't stand in front of the mirror for two hours gluing everything down. They just got up and went to work!

The props don't look right either.

What I mean by that is, all the props that they use have been collected over the years... Props from the 1950s in this case, which means although they are authentic, they now look old.

The problem with that is, they wouldn't have looked old in the 1950s would they, because they would have all been new? So what we've actually got today is, a group of perfectly dressed and groomed bunch of people, being filmed in what can only be described as a modern day museum.

By the way, I've just been told to take my doctor's white coat off, just in case it gets creased... See what I mean?

There's also a tendency to glamour things up on some of the big TV period dramas as well. This means that not only have you got immaculately dressed people with perfectly styled hair, you've also got gorgeous looking women and chisel faced hunks, all posing around the camera, like it's an *Hello Magazine* photo shoot.

ITV have just started to air *Victoria* which is a period drama based on the life of Queen Victoria. It's basically about a Kate Moss lookalike, living in a big posh castle! It's all too razzmatazz for me.

The thing is, I want it to be as real as possible. I want normal-looking people, who have dressed as if they have dressed normally and not spent hours in costume. I want to see Queen Victoria as she was and not as she wasn't.

You would have thought that we'd have learnt over the years when dishing out this kind of rubbish, but we haven't. We've just carried on the tradition.

I was flicking through the channels the other day and happened to stumble across an old Robin Hood film.

I'd joined the action where Robin was sitting around a camp fire. He'd been camped out in the woods with his merry men, as they were hiding from the Sheriff of Nottingham.

He was just about to throw a log on the fire, when all of a sudden Maid Marion appeared from behind a bush, lips thick with Rimmel and a face full of Max Factor.

She'd also managed to find an hair salon from somewhere, as her hair was curled beautifully. Either that or she'd taken a set of curling tongs in there with her.

Robin Hood meanwhile looked like he'd just jumped off a sunbed, or recently returned from a fortnight in Majorca. He certainly didn't look like he'd been camping out in the forest for the past six months, that was for sure.

I've only got to be caravanning in Barmouth for three days and look like I've been dragged through a hedge backwards. My hair looking like it's never seen a comb! Not Robin though. He'd got perfect hair, perfect sideburns and it was all jelled to perfection.

So there you have it, which is a good job really, because it looks like I'm on next. My walk past the camera is almost upon me.

Unfortunately my perfectly jelled hair, which was moulded into place, following 30 minutes of careful strategic planning, regrettably will not be making an appearance today…

Wardrobe have just covered it up with a hat!

WHAT I DO IN PUBLIC TOILETS

I don't know about you, but I like a bit of privacy when I go and sit on the great white elephant. Unfortunately this can be a bit of a problem when I'm not at home.

Most toilets are a no-go area for me when I'm out and about. They are too confined, too intimate and too public. Put it this way... If there's a gap at the bottom of the trap, then forget it.

I very often use the disabled facilities, because you've basically got your own room. You're totally cut off. You've got your own sink, hand drier, you can hang your coat up and you can make as much noise as you like (if you want to that is)

Most disabled toilets are tucked away down a corridor, so you can usually sneak in with no one noticing, but sometimes you will find that they are not. Sometimes they can be in full view of Customer Services (especially in some Sainsbury's) This can be very awkward, especially if the store is particularly quiet and all they've got to do is stare at you.

What I tend to do if I ever find myself in this situation, is put on a bit of a limp, because at least then it sort of justifies the reason why you're going in there in the first place.

This basically covers me and saves me from any awkward questions, when I'm on my way out.

I would much rather do this than have to sit and witness the strains of a man, who is sitting just a few inches away in the next cubicle. A man who had obviously had a dodgy vindaloo the night before.

The design of the traps don't help either, as the sight of his trousers round his ankles is plain to see and because you are so close, the grunts, farts and splashes are unfortunately all at full volume.

Even standing at one of the urinals, staring at an advertisement about life cover can have its problems too. Not only have you got to deal with all the sound effects coming from trap two, but you've also got to deal with the bloke who is standing next to you, desperately trying to aim straight with one hand, while trying to make a phone call or text with the other.

It's all very primitive and not something that I usually partake in.

Going to the toilet for me is very much a private affair and do not want to share that experience with anyone else, especially a complete stranger who is determined to let the whole world know he's pebble dashing the place.

So it's the disabled toilet all the way for me. It's peace of mind, knowing that all my toilet manoeuvres will be done in private and in comfort.

Disabled toilets are security friendly too, whereas a public toilet is a free for all. A public toilet means any nutcase can just waltz in and invade your space, and that's exactly what happened to me the other week, when I was in Sainsbury's.

Unfortunately I was caught short and needed to use the toilet. To my horror an 'Out of Order' sign had been pinned to the disabled toilet's door. This meant that my only option was to go against the grain and use the communal one. There was good news though, because as I entered, the absence of men was plain to see. The urinals were empty and there were no grunts or groans coming from any of the traps.

I stood at the wall and began to relieve myself, trying my hardest to be as quick as possible. This is where the security issue arises.

Suddenly I heard the door open. I glanced across my shoulder and in walked a grubby looking man. He smelt like what I can only describe as horse manure.

He walked over, stood next to me, dropped everything to his ankles, took his shirt off and started to grunt!

It was absolutely disgusting! No one should ever have to share a room with a man in soiled underpants! This is a problem that obviously doesn't occur when using the disabled facilities.

The good news is most places now have them, so it's quite easy to find yourself your own bit of space, whenever the need arises.

Life is not about putting up with things. If there's an easier option, then you have to go for it and that applies to public toilets too.

Why struggle, when you can have a room of your own?

WE'VE BEEN HERE HOW LONG?

The world has been around for over 4.5 billion years and humans have been around for 200 thousand years, yet 150 years ago, we were living in squalor and crapping in the gutter. Surely if we have been here that long, wouldn't we have worked it all out a lot sooner than that?

The trouble is, how do we really know what happened before we were here anyway? We are only repeating and passing onto another generation, what people have passed on to us. It's only what we've been told by somebody else. It could all just be a big wind up!

My dad has a tendency to exaggerate. He just can't help it, it just happens.

If someone tells him that a car cost them £10,000 there's a good chance it will be £12,000 by the time he gets home. A £3 million lottery win becomes £5 million, a 45-minute wait at the doctors becomes two hours, and he once drank a pint of bull's blood in 1958… But did he?

The thing is, what if my dad had lived in the thirteenth century? Just think how many tales he could have exaggerated in his lifetime? All this information could have then been written down and then passed onto the next generation of exaggerators.

Nine hundred and fifty years ago, William II was shot in the New Forest by an arrow, but was he?

On April 22nd 1500 Pedro Alverez Cabral discovered Brazil, but did he? Even if he did, wasn't it there already?

We need to take history with a pinch of salt, because at the end of the day, do we really know the truth?

As I am writing this chapter, NASA's new Horizons spacecraft has finally reached Pluto, after ten years from its initial launch.

It has started to beam back pictures now and guess what? Pluto is a lot bigger than was first thought! See what I mean? The information about Pluto is forever changing and will no doubt change again in the coming months and years that follow.

That can probably be said about the Earth too. Four and a half billion years old at the moment, 5.5 billion years old next year... Who knows?

So what if we believe what the scientists say and the Earth is 4.5 billion years old?

What does the Bible say about it?

Well, there have been many Bible scholars over the years that have tried to work this one out and the general belief seems to hover around about the 6000 years mark. A bit of a difference isn't there?

This can obviously leave you in a bit of a dilemma if you are religious, because if the earth was created 4.5 billion years ago, what actually did God create?

If you do choose to go down the Bible route, you must then decide whether you believe in dinosaurs or not, because apparently dinosaurs were here nearly 200 million years before that!

Scientists divulge very precise information about these types of things, with dinosaurs being at the very top of the list.

A dinosaur bone has recently been discovered in South America. They have determined that the bone is precisely 101.6 billion years old and think that they may even know what its heart rate was.

Now I'm quite willing to accept the fact that at some point in time, dinosaurs did actually exist, but for someone to tell me a dinosaur that lived 4.3 billion years ago's heart rate was 140 over 84 is taking it a little bit too far as far as I'm concerned.

We get fed this information all the time, but it doesn't mean we have to believe it.

Apparently dinosaurs became extinct about 65.5 million years ago, but trying to pinpoint the exact reason for this, is very difficult and you won't be surprised to learn that scientists have several theories.

One theory is that small mammals ate dinosaur eggs until there were none left… Honest!

Other scientists believe the cause was dinosaur's bodies becoming too big for their brains.

Others believe climate change, and on and on it goes. Many scientists, with varying opinions, all using words like about, believe, estimate, speculate, maybe, could have, and 'we don't really know really, but we could be right' type of words.

I wonder what has been discovered today?

Probably a human handprint that's 110 million years old… Oh they have!

THE PERILS OF KNOCKING ON A BIT

When you're a younger man and you're going out for the evening, it's usually a quick shave, a wash and you're out.

When you get older though, you have to contend with a 30-minute pruning session, before you can even contemplate reaching for the soap. You suddenly find that you've got hair everywhere! Everywhere except for where it's supposed to be that is… i.e. on your head.

Isn't it strange…? You've got a bushy mop of hair one minute and then you're holding onto every strand of hair possible the next. Your ears meanwhile have got Sherwood Forest growing out of them, with your nostrils not too far behind.

You've also got your eyebrows to deal with. They are growing that fast, a daily trim suddenly starts to feel inadequate

Also the moles on your neck have started sprouting as well, which has resulted in even more work in the daily pruning department.

But even though you've got all this going on, the hair on your head refuses to grow, and continues to become that barren landscape, where hair once lived and thrived, but where it now struggles to survive.

Remembering things can also be a problem as you get older, but have you ever thought why this is?

People automatically think that it could be the early signs of Alzheimer's setting in and it could be, but have you ever thought that it could just simply be a case of lack of storage? Think about it.

If you're young, you haven't got that much to remember have you? Unlike a 50 year old… He's got to store away 50 years of memories and that's a long time and an awful lot to store away. You haven't just got 15 years to remember, you've got 50!

This only gets worse with age, as your storage slowly fills up with even more information.

It's not as if your brain gets any bigger is it? You can't just upgrade your brain and get more storage like you can with your computer, or your iCloud account.

But does all that matter anyway?

Does it really matter if you can't remember everything?

Remembering just the important stuff is what really matters. Luckily that will be safely tucked away in your memory banks.

This means that remembering what colour cardigan your geography teacher had on in 1975 is no longer relevant. You will find that that piece of trivial information is gone and was probably sent to your brain's recycle bin in about 1984.

I think that in time your own body decides which memories are worth keeping and which memories need deleting, so I don't think you should get too stressed out if you can't remember what your favourite trousers were in 1981.

Recently, I was added to a group on Facebook. It was my old school (apparently).

The strange thing is, most of the posts that were on there didn't seem to have any relevance to me at all. I couldn't recognise anyone, I couldn't remember any of the school trips that they enthusiastically spoke about, I wasn't in any of the photographs and I couldn't comment on any of the activities that were mentioned, because I couldn't remember any of them.

"Are you sure I went to this school?" I posted.

"Still the joker, Stuart?" came the reply by someone called Dave – to this day, I still have no idea who he is.

Luckily, I have recently spotted at least three people on there that I can remember and two more who vaguely look familiar.

I can only put this memory loss down to the fact that I was doing much more exciting things at the time, and as I didn't like school at all, my brain decided to delete most of it when I left.

Another reason could be because of my creative mind. Creative minds don't tend to get cluttered up with trivial things that don't really matter and obviously school must have been one of those trivial things.

Whatever the reason, I can't remember much about it anyway.

I can tell you one thing though.

If anyone mentions the geography teacher's cardigan on Facebook again, I will pull my hair out!

Well, I would if I'd got some of course.

DON'T BE FOOLED BY THE SMILING WOMAN IN A BOWLING T-SHIRT

If you happen to have kids and they suddenly become interested in some kind of leisure activity, then please be prepared for the worst.

I made the grave mistake of taking my eight-year-old son bowling once. He really wanted to go, so sure enough, off we went to our local bowling alley.

We'd only been there ten minutes when all of a sudden a lady in a brightly coloured T-shirt came over, smiled and said: "We've got a bowling club here you know. It's every Saturday morning. It's only £2 a week and they get four hours bowling. Do you think he might want to join?"

I looked down at my son, who was very excited at the prospect of bowling for four hours every Saturday and, as this particular session had cost me £5.95 for just the one hour, I thought that it was probably a good idea for him to give it a go, so I agreed.

The chirpy woman smiled, handed my son his spanking brand-new paper membership card and then scurried off to find herself another victim.

The first Saturday arrived and sure enough it was exactly what the lady had said... £2 which I paid on arrival.

My son excitedly changed into his bowling shoes and then headed off to partake in his four hour bowling fest at just 50p per hour.

This was a perfect time for me to relax.

I fetched a coffee and then settled down to do some writing... 'Bliss,' I thought.

Within five minutes though, the lady who had originally asked me to join came over for a chat.

"It's lovely to see you here," she said grinning. "Fancy a lottery ticket?"

Basically what she had done was to make up some fake lottery tickets with just one number on, and if that number matched the bonus ball on the main lottery, you won a prize.

"It's only a pound," she said. "The winner gets a bottle of wine, with all the money raised going towards the club's annual trip to Blackpool."

Fair enough I thought. It's only a pound and at least it's going to something all the kids can enjoy, even though they may not even want to go to Blackpool.

She'd only been gone five minutes, when all of a sudden, a voice from behind me said: "Fancy a raffle ticket?"

I turned round and standing there, was a large man in a bowling cap. He had a book in one hand and a pen in the other.

"Pound a strip, mate" he said, as he automatically ripped out two.

"We're trying to raise enough money to get the bowling team to the North West competition in Manchester."

At this point the alarm bells had started to go off. I'd already spent £5 and I'd only been in there 15 minutes.

Next came the woman with the fruit basket.

"We're collecting for Brenda," she said, as she held out a brightly coloured collection tin. "It's her birthday on Wednesday and we thought that it would be nice if we all chipped in and got her something."

'Who is this Brenda,' I thought? Was she one of the bowlers mum's? One of the grandmas? The tea lady maybe? Who was she?

Well, apparently she was a woman that lived across the road from the bowling alley who occasionally turned up to have a look… And that was it!

It didn't stop there either.

I was soon confronted by a man holding a football card, a woman collecting for someone's up-and-coming wedding and another woman in a bobble hat, trying to get £1.50 off me towards the Christmas Party.

Luckily for me, my son wasn't too impressed with his new Saturday morning pastime, so we decided to knock the bowling on the head and not return.

So beware folks of leisure activities for kids. Don't get sucked in and if someone does approach you smiling, offering a cheap Saturday morning pastime for your child… Do the sensible thing. Turn and run!

CAN WE HAVE OUR FIELDS BACK PLEASE?

I hate it when I see a field being built on. I hate it because I know that that field will never be a field again.

Even in years to come, when the warehouse that was built on that field is no longer required, you won't see that field returning. It will lay dormant, until such a time when some property developer turns up to build 500 kennels on there, complete with no garden, no drive, and a brick wall for a view. Whatever the outcome, the one thing you can guarantee it won't be, will be a field again.

It makes me sad when a field is vandalised in this way.

Sometimes buildings become derelict, on land that was once a beautiful field. These buildings can very often sit inactive for years. Nobody seems to want them and the authorities seem to be at a loss as to know what to do with them, so why not just turn them back into what they were before?

Unfortunately this not going to happen, is it? When did you ever hear of a local authority giving planning permission for a field...? Once it's gone I'm afraid, it's gone!

New roads and motorways are a big concern as far as losing fields are concerned too, but an even bigger concern is where the junctions will be placed, because junctions mean even more field vandalisation.

A junction is like a seed. A seed that will slowly grow and grow. It may just start off as a service area or a Premier Inn, but it won't be too long before a retail park is attached, followed by an housing development and before you know it, the field that once was will be gone, and the junction where the seed was planted will have grown and amalgamated into the nearest town.

A new road appeared a few miles away from us about five years ago and the junction seeds were planted as per usual.

Unfortunately, the fields between two of the junctions have now almost vanished and instead of picking strawberries straight from a field like we used to do, we now pick them straight from a newly built Tesco's instead.

My mum grew up in Kent and I had some lovely holidays when I used to go back with her and spend time with my nan and granddad.

They lived in a village just outside Ashford and I can remember vividly walking into the back garden and then going for lovely walks across the fields.

It was so picturesque. We picked fruit as we walked. It was real *Darling Buds of May* country… An unspoilt paradise.

I went back a few years ago. Twenty years had lapsed since I was there last and the change was absolutely catastrophic.

The fields had gone, the hedgerows had gone, the fruit had gone, and the deafening silence had gone. It had all been replaced by noise, pollution and concrete.

The back of my nan and granddad's house where we used to sit shelling peas was unrecognisable. Instead of overlooking miles and miles of fields, it now overlooked industrial estates and a motorway. The garden of England had been concreted over!

In just 20 years it had disappeared and that beautiful landscape that was, was gone forever, never to be recreated again.

The sad thing is, the locals used to cherish the area and their way of life. Their community was strong and they looked after the land. Land that was meant to be passed on to future generations, but there's nothing left. The area is dead and the industrial estates and roads have taken over.

Forget that quiet walk across the fields picking blackberries, it's now a noisy walk past Screwfix on a littered A2070.

The walk along the stream, the picnics next to the wood, the cobnuts, the orchards, the miles and miles of adventure have all gone and will never return.

DO YOU WANT ANY HELP WITH YOUR PACKING?

Those are the immortal words you hear every time you finish your weekly shop, but are they sincere? Does this supermarket checkout assistant really want to help you with your packing, or is it an indication that you have just been confronted by a checkout robot on autopilot?

The trouble is, all supermarkets program their staff in exactly the same way, so there's no real getting away from it.

To be on the safe side you should always say no to this question, because saying yes could result in half a dozen sea scouts turning up to fight over it, and unless you want your washing up liquid ending up with your frozen chips, then saying no really is the only safe option.

The other week I decided to visit my local Sainsbury's to carry out what I call 'a checkout robot assessment' and I was not disappointed by the outcome.

As I watched my shopping slowly travel along the conveyor belt, I noticed the young checkout assistant, carefully starting to prepare four carrier bags, in readiness for her first question.

Suddenly she hit me with it!

"Do you want any help with your packing?" she said as two cartons of apple juice came to a grinding halt.

"No, I'm fine thanks" I replied, as I lay in wait.

Unfortunately this did not deter the girl and it wasn't too long, before she quickly stepped up a gear, by hitting me with three in a row.

"Do you have a rewards card?" Do you collect the school vouchers?" And "Would you like any cash back?"

Another frustrating phrase that you have to endure at the checkout is:

"Can you enter your PIN please?"

Then when you have entered it, they will hit you with "Would you like to remove your card?"

What's all that about? Sometimes I feel like saying,

"No you're okay, I think I'll leave it in there all day".

Occasionally the assistant will ask you to remove your card, even before the machine wants you to. This I find really frustrating.

Sometimes just for a laugh, I'll remove the card before I'm even asked.

One girl was that much into her checkout routine once, that she completely got carried away and asked me to enter my PIN, just as I was handing over the cash. She then said,

"Have a nice day," and quickly followed it up with "Do you want any help with your packing?" which was obviously intended for her next customer.

A few weeks ago, a lady was at the checkout waiting to pay for a fake leather handbag. It all seemed quite straightforward at the time; a bag on a conveyor belt and a customer all ready to make a payment, but a real pantomime was about to get underway.

The checkout assistant picked the bag up, scanned it and then went through her usual 'Do you want any help with your packing?' routine.

Unfortunately, the customer said yes.

This meant that for the next five minutes, I had to watch and endure this assistant, frustratingly try and get a fake leather handbag into a carrier bag, which was an impossibility, as both bags were exactly the same size.

Fortunately for me and everyone else in the queue, the customer changed her mind, which was a relief to us all, as we could have been in there all afternoon.

Another woman, who was at the opposite checkout, had purchased a box of Rice Krispies and a packet of organic bananas. All of a sudden, she went into a frantic frenzy, when she suddenly realised she couldn't find her rewards' card.

It was a matter of life or death, as she frantically emptied the whole contents of her handbag all over the checkout.

But why was this woman in such a state of emergency?

Well, it's because she thinks she's being rewarded for loyalty, but in fact all that's happened is she has lost her Sainsbury's identity card. It's Sainsbury's that should be panicking and not her.

Supermarkets just want to keep a tabs on what you are buying and which store you are buying it from. This means that if your weekly shop is full of Kellogg's and McVitie's, then you shouldn't be too surprised to find money-off vouchers for Crunchy Nut Cornflakes and McVitie's Ginger Nuts, dropping through your letterbox a couple of weeks later.

"Do you want any help with your packing?" Good Luck!

FANCY AN EXPENSIVE DAY OUT?

The kids wanted to go to Alton Towers today and then go for a pizza on the way home, but after checking out the prices, I thought it would be a much better idea all round, if we all went for a picnic instead.

Picnics are great! You choose the food, you choose where to have them and it doesn't cost you nearly £200 to have one.

These days it costs so much to take a family out, even just for a couple of hours.

We were out shopping last week and there was an ice-cream stand inside the shopping centre. I asked the girl how much it would be for four small ice creams.

"Nine pounds," she replied.

I pointed out that I had no intentions in buying the whole supply of ice-cream and that I just wanted four cones.

She looked at me, smiled and then confirmed that this extortionate £9 price was in fact the price of four small ice creams.

This obviously led to the ice-cream stand losing a sale, which meant that this particular transaction failed to materialise.

The same applies to teashops.

Call in somewhere for tea and cakes and you'll be lucky to get any change from a £20 note.

One place we visited wanted £2 for a cup of tea!

"You can have a larger cup for £2.50," she said, as I stood there gazing at the price list.

Did I really want to pay an extra 50p for just an extra drop of hot water though? Err, no!

At the end of the day, a cup of tea is basically a cup of boiling water, with a tea bag dropped in. All she was offering was a bigger cup.

"We can do a pot of tea for two for £3.50," she said, as I stood there in shock.

This amazing offer of a pot of tea for two, consisted of a pot of boiling water with two tea bags dropped in, which to me was exactly the same as two cups of tea, except this time it was in a pot, which we were paying an extra pound for.

"How much would it be for a pot of tea and four custard tarts?" I asked.

She took a quick glance at her price list, looked up and said, "£14".

Now I know a cafe has overheads, but it has almost become impossible now for a family to go out and enjoy just simple pleasures.

So what about popping into the supermarket cafe then after doing your weekly shop? Surely it can't be expensive in there... Can it?

Well, take a family of four in for a drink and a pack of biscuits each and you'll soon find that it certainly is. I ended up paying £14.51 for two coffees, one bottle of water, an orange juice and four digestives. It doesn't matter if you're on your own, because you're only paying for yourself, but when you're a family and poor old dad's got to fork out, then it becomes a completely different ball game all together.

What I'm trying to say is. If a single person goes out and has a drink and two biscuits, he or she will only pay for a drink and two biscuits, but if I go out and have a drink and two biscuits, I end up paying for four drinks and four biscuits, even though I am consuming exactly the same as the single person is.

This brings me back to the subject of theme parks and although it's bad enough taking your family to one, it's even worse when a single person tags along too.

Firstly, I'm the breadwinner, which means I will have to pay up to four times more entrance fee than my friend will, as he only has himself to worry about.

A family ticket will of course get me a slight reduction, but it's nothing to shout home about, as the extra £10 off, will soon be swallowed up by the first purchase of a Coke at £2.50 each.

Your friend, meanwhile, is quid's in, as he's only had to buy a single Fanta.

Then comes the ice creams, another Coke, chips and even more Coke as the expense of the day continues to rocket.

An evening meal on the way home is the final nail in the coffin, as you suddenly realise a fortnight in Majorca would have worked out a damn sight cheaper.

The other week we went to a wedding. It was another one of those forced fun occasions, but we went anyway.

Unfortunately it was held up at some big posh castle and was one of those weddings where it costs you an arm and a leg just to breathe. A small bottle of beer was £6 and a glass of pineapple juice was £3.80.

There was some good news though. Fortunately the kids weren't with us, as they hadn't been invited. If they had, then I would have got straight back in the car and taken them to the nearest theme park.

So what do you do, if you're the one that pays for everything?

That's simple. Either take them for a picnic, or go out on your own. You'll find it's a damn sight cheaper.

I'M SICK TO THE BACK TEETH OF ENTHUSIASTS

When I'm going somewhere in my car, I do occasionally expect to be held up by the odd bit of congested traffic (i.e. traffic accident or road works) but when I get held up by some kind of enthusiasts event, then I'm not an happy man at all.

This is exactly what happened to me last week, on what I thought was going to be a relatively routine car journey to Shrewsbury, on a lovely quiet Sunday morning, but instead turned out to be a complete nightmare.

Generally this trip would be a simple routine operation.

It would usually involve me cruising along the M54 at a steady 70 mph (not a whiff of a traffic jam anywhere) and then turn up in Shrewsbury, 40 minutes later, relaxed and stress free.

Unfortunately this week proved not to be the case, and within just two minutes of my journey I was suddenly confronted by a mass of flashing hazard lights and miles of stationary traffic.

So why had my usually quiet, quaint, car-free motorway, suddenly become a car park?

Well I was just about to find out, because traffic police were walking between the cars, notifying drivers of the problems that lay ahead, and the good news was that one of them was heading towards me.

'Maybe it's an overturned lorry,' I thought, 'or maybe a caravan has jack-knifed and has blocked the lanes. Maybe it's a multiple vehicle pileup?' It didn't look good whatever it was.

A grim looking traffic cop approached my window. I wound it down.

"Sorry for the delay, sir," said the policeman "It's the motorcyclist enthusiasts' club. They're having a get-together, so we've had to close off the next junction AND the A41" And off he went to spread his doom and gloom to the rest of the drivers behind me.

The thing is, why should thousands of people who have no interest in motorcycles at all, be held up for hours on a motorway, just because a few dozen motorcycle enthusiasts want to swan around on their play things?

The same happened a few weeks ago in Worcester. I was held up for over an hour by a flower show…! Honestly.

Basically flower enthusiasts (about 30 of them) decided that they wanted to meet up in a field and show off their daffodils to each other.

This is all very well, but when half of Worcestershire is held up on the A4440 because of it, I think they really need to think about the anarchy that they are causing.

At the end of the day, being enthusiastic over something, shouldn't affect anybody else who isn't.

A friend of mine is a stamp collector. It's obviously not everyone's cup of tea, but it is to him and he absolutely loves it.

He doesn't need to inconvenience anybody else to do it though. You won't find him sat on the M54 flicking through his stamp collection, and you certainly won't see him closing off any A-roads, just because he wants to show his replica Penny Black off to a few of his mates.

Last year I was held up on the outskirts of Wolverhampton for almost 45 minutes, just because a fun run was being held.

I'm sorry, but an handful of people running around in shorts, should NOT be allowed to bring the whole of Wolverhampton to a standstill.

If you're a runner, then please find yourself a running track. If you're a motorcyclist, then please find yourself a racing track, AND if you like growing flowers, then please do us all a favour and stop in your bloody greenhouse.

GOING ON MY NHS APPLE HUNT

Usually the first thing that greets you in the waiting room of an NHS establishment these days, is a television. Generally, it's stuck to a wall trying to sell us something.

The trouble is, when you are feeling ill, the last thing you want is Michael Parkinson rabbling on about medical insurance.

Last year I had to rush my dad to the accident and emergency department at our local city hospital, as he'd decided to hack the end of his finger off while trying to prune a bush. I dropped him off and then went and sat in the waiting room.

The room I found myself in had the usual flat screen television, strategically placed in the centre of the wall. There were rows of us all looking up staring at it. It felt more like Cineworld than A&E and to be honest a nice box of popcorn wouldn't have gone amiss.

How to plan for your retirement was the first action-packed screening. Apparently all my worries will be over, if I agree to pay £50 a month for it.

Medical insurance was also on offer at £25 a month and to top it off, I could have new windows fitted for as little as

£2,500 by simply ringing a convenient free phone number. Not only that, but I could even pay for them over five years as well.

I'd only been sat down three minutes and already I was on the verge of paying out £75 per month insurance and two and half grand on new windows.

I was then riveted to my chair, as I sat through some very interesting facts about water.

It was basically informing me that it was better for me to drink a bottle of water, than 15 pints of lager… Really?

The main feature though, amazingly enough, was all about healthy eating. It showed a lovely picture of an apple and it urged everyone to steer away from crisps, chocolates, sugary drinks, pasties and pies.

After an hour of waiting and watching the same five minute loop about insurance, windows, doors and various other types of claptrap, I decided to go on a quest.

I was feeling a little bit peckish and so decided to take up the hospitals advice and go and fetch myself an apple.

As I entered the corridor, I spotted a vending machine, but was then saddened to find that the only item that resembled anything remotely like an apple was a wrapped up green sugary square in a packet of starburst.

Someone then kindly advised me that there was a shop in the next corridor, so excitedly I headed off in search for my healthy hospital treat.

When I reached the shop, it was situated next to the heart ward and after checking out the merchandise, I reckon it probably played a big part in putting most of them in there.

The shop itself was floor to ceiling crisps one side, and chocolate and sweets the other. I did ask the assistant if she had any apples in stock, but she just stared at me as if I'd just arrived from another planet. I was not deterred though and was resolute in finding my apple, which the hospital had urged I eat only five minutes before.

As I reached the end of the hospital corridor, I was horrified to see that Greggs had moved in, complete with hordes of doctors and nurses all sitting around eating pies.

One doctor had just demolished a pasty and was in the process of knocking back a packet of salt & vinegar Monster Munch.

Another doctor was devouring a large sausage roll, while intermittently swigging on a bottle of Pepsi.

Two nurses were in the corner, brushing flakes of pastry off their uniforms, as they prepared to polish off a couple of king-sized Kit Kats.

Everywhere you looked there were medical professionals, all guzzling themselves silly on all things Greggs.

I approached the counter, but it was all in vain… It was apple-less.

I decided that it was time to bring my apple hunt to a conclusion, as finding one seemed an impossibility.

I headed back to the A&E Department, emptying a packet of cheese & onion crisps from the vending machine on my way through.

Unfortunately hospitals have now been infiltrated by huge companies, selling unhealthy food.

Currently there are over 130 NHS hospitals occupied by fast food outlets such as McDonald's, Burger King and Subway.

Maybe they should stick a McDonald's outside the maternity ward here? They could then treat their new-born to its very first happy meal.

WHAT'S THE FASCINATION OF NESTING IN WALSALL?

Why do some birds live in run down areas?
Why do some birds live in a tree, surrounded by sweet-wrappers and beer cans?

Why would a bird want to live in a bush, next to a busy main road, in a city suburb in between KFC and a Burger King... Why?

If I was a bird, I'd soon be off.

I'd be lapping it up in Cornwall, or a picturesque village on the Welsh coast. I certainly wouldn't be trying to set up a nest in the middle of Walsall that's for sure.

Not only have you got to deal with the noise, the pollution and all the yobs in Walsall, but you've also got to take into account the overwhelming population of cats.

I noticed a nest last week. It was high up in a tree and was sandwiched in between a petrol station and a rundown pub. Surrounding it was a huge housing estate. An housing estate that doesn't just have cats, but an housing estate where cats hang around in gangs. Hundreds of them, prowling the streets, terrorising wild life. It really isn't the sort of place where a bird should be living.

Why not find a field in Shropshire, where the nearest moggy is five miles away? Why live in such a dire and dangerous place? It just doesn't make sense to me.

Why not head off to the coast? It's not as if they've got to walk is it? They can fly, and fly pretty fast too.

This certainly rings true where ducks are concerned.

Ducks are surprisingly fast flyers at 60 mph, which means a duck could be in Barmouth in no time at all. This is why I'm bemused about the ducks in our local park.

Why would half a dozen ducks choose to hang out in a dirty pond, surrounded by empty crisp packets, when they could be lapping it up in a park by the sea? Like all the rest of inner city birds, they just don't seem to get it.

I am of course well aware that urban life is an attractive food-rich environment, but even so, is it really worth living in a noisy, polluted suburb, with an 80% chance of being eaten by a cat? I don't think it is and on that basis, I'd be off like a flash, living in a village by the coast, as soon as it was physically possible for me to leave the nest. It's just not worth risking your life over. Just for a few crumbs and the occasional peck at a fat ball.

Don't get me wrong, everywhere has its dangers, but I would rather risk dodging three or four foxes, than be hounded 24-hours a day, by inner-city cat street gangs.

What birds have to remember is…

Cats are limited to where they can go. Yes, they are very independent, but they will never be too far away from their bowl of Kitty Kat.

Birds on the other hand have no restrictions whatsoever. They can go absolutely anywhere they want, which is why for the life of me, I cannot understand why they don't.

Living by the sea, up a tree in a cat-free zone would definitely be the way forward for me!

I'd nip down to the beach every morning (when was the last time you saw a cat on a beach?), have a nice stroll, pick up the odd chip, a quick fly above the waves, a trip into town and then head back to my tree for a nice afternoon kip... A Walsall bird meanwhile, will be hid behind a KFC container, trying it's hardest not to be devoured by the moggy from number ten.

DON'T WASTE TIME DOING SOMETHING THAT DOESN'T NEED DOING

We have three taps in the house and a shower that drips…

"That tap's dripping again in the kitchen," my wife will say, as she looks across at me with a 'isn't it about time you sorted that tap out' kind of a look on her face.

The thing is, yes it does drip, but if it's turned off in the way that I have demonstrated, then it will not.

The same applies to the two taps in the bathroom, which also don't drip, if turned off when the correct technique is carried out.

She would obviously like them all fixed, but why fix something that doesn't really need fixing yet?

The whole idea of a tap is to turn on water and turn off water and as far as I'm concerned, that's exactly what they do, so what's the urgency?

The dripping shower is a little bit more trickier than the taps, because once you've turned the shower off, you then have to clamber under the cupboard and turn a screw to the left, with a screwdriver that I have conveniently left in a bowl next to the pipe. Sometimes the shower will continue to drip, but this is purely because whoever turned the screw, hasn't turned it to the left enough.

My main point is the shower still works as a shower and can still be turned off (just like the taps) if the correct procedure is undertaken.

What I'm trying to say in this chapter is: You don't have to waste time doing something that doesn't really need doing.

There are many examples in day to day life, of people wasting valuable time fixing things that already work and buying things that they already have. It's all a waste of time and it's time that can be put to better use.

I was chatting away to a friend the other day and as we were chatting, she suddenly came out with, "We could do with a new kitchen table and chairs".

Now bear in mind that we were sitting in her house, in the kitchen AND at the table. The table had four legs and was doing exactly what a table is designed to do.

The chairs were also working normally, yet she was convinced that a new set of table and chairs were needed.

She was sitting there plotting a plan, which involved dragging her poor husband around the furniture shops on the following Saturday, in the hope of finding something that she already had! A whole day wasted!

Good job she hasn't got a dripping tap, because that would have been his Sunday morning gone as well, or the whole day if he lived in my house.

The thing is you could literally spend weeks, months and years fixing things that work already and at the same time spend a fortune on various items that you've already got.

People even replace small everyday items that don't need replacing. A mug with a chip, a saucepan with a slightly dented lid, a broken chain on a bath plug, they all work, but they still replace them.

What about things that we buy, but we never use, but yet still keep us busy?

At the moment, my wife is in the garden struggling with a ten-foot plastic greenhouse that she erected five years ago.

Unfortunately a storm last night caused one of the polythene sides to rip and so she is now out there in the pouring rain, trying to repair it with a very large roll of sticky tape.

I'd also like to point out that there is nothing actually in the greenhouse that is garden related and there hasn't been for over two years.

The thing is, if she hadn't have bought the greenhouse in the first place, then she wouldn't be out there now, soaking wet, trying to save something that is currently storing half a dozen empty paint tins, a rusty can of WD-40 and an empty box of Celebrations, that is full of assorted woodscrews and various Rawlplugs.

We waste so much time fixing and replacing things. It's all an unnecessary hassle, that we can well do without.

We can save a hell of a lot of time doing away with things that we don't use and stop doing things around the house that simply don't need doing.

Our kitchen is a great example of this.

In there we have two spotlight fittings that both take three RO95 BC lamps. These lamps cost £3 each, so as you can imagine it can be very expensive when they start to go. Replace one and before you know it, another one's gone and then another and then another.

Fortunately for me, four of the lamp holders have burnt out and have welded themselves to the base of the previous lamps, which means we now only have two left that actually work (one in each fitting).

To most people this would be a disaster, but as far as I'm concerned, it's a real money-saver, with constant lamp changing now a thing of the past.

As far as lighting up the kitchen is concerned, this is also not a problem as they are the good old fashioned 100w RO95s, which means they are so bright, any football stadium in the land would be proud to have them.

Unfortunately this is not the case for our friends, who have recently had new state-of-the-art light fittings fitted in their kitchen.

These new fittings use the new £8 at a time energy-saver lamps and although there are 12 of them in total, you still find yourself fumbling around looking for the kettle, once night time falls.

So I am happy to stick with my two RO95s thank you very much, until the day I discover they have also welded themselves to the light fitting.

Busy Doing Nothing

Open up your eyes
There's another day ahead
Of you busy doing nothing
Before you get back to bed

Then it starts all over again
Of doing more of the same
Just busy doing nothing
But there's no one else to blame

Because it's all down to you
But it's something you can't see
Because you're busy doing nothing
And it really is nothing, believe me

So take this as a warning
If you don't hear this plea
You'll always be busy doing nothing
Instead of doing nothing, like me!

SMILE, YOU'RE ON CAMERA

I had a very important meeting in London today, but before venturing off on my journey, I made sure that my hair was washed, my best clobber was ironed and that I'd had a nice bath.

I really wanted to look my best, because of the endless amount of cameras that I was about to encounter.

You probably think that it sounds exciting being in the public eye and that I would love to absorb all the attention and limelight, but regrettably I'm not talking about a ritzy day out at a film premiere, I'm talking about the immeasurable intrusion into my privacy and yours.

My day of stardom began right from the off.

I walked out of the house, locked the door, headed towards my car and then glanced up. A Google van was heading down the street and the camera was pointing at me. I gave it a little wave as I opened the driver's door.

Then as I lowered myself into the car seat I noticed the next-door neighbour's security camera manoeuvring from side to side, like a little robot, as it followed my every move.

Already I was starting to feel slightly paranoid, as I pulled off the drive and headed down the street.

So what happened on my journey?

Well I've got to say, I was a real megastar on my 120-mile trip down to the big smoke.

I drove through CCTV cameras up to junction 10, average speed check cameras on the M6, M42, M40, traffic control cameras, safety cameras, the list was endless.

When I eventually did reach my destination on the outskirts of London, I was really relieved to park up, relax and take a bit of a breather from my hectic filming schedule.

As I got out of the car though, a man looking a little bit concerned walked over and asked me if I knew if we were in the congestion zone or not?

"I don't think so," I said, as I tried to recall the road signs on my approach in.

As the man scurried off in a bit of a panic, I decided to go into a nearby shop and inquire for myself. 'Surely I would have noticed,' I thought.

The man in the shop informed me that if I had driven under the bridge opposite, then I was most definitely in the congestion zone.

I decided to take a stroll down the road and inspect the bridge in question.

I looked up… There was no getting away from it; there were four fixed cameras above the road to catch my every move.

'Where were the "dumb us down" signs when I needed some?' I thought.

I looked at the congestion zone sign. It was roughly the size of a postage stamp, yet the sign informing me that I was approaching a bridge, was as nearly as big as the bridge itself. This sign was obviously not needed, as anyone with anything sandwiched in between their ears, would have instantly realised that the arched brick construction in front of them, was probably a big enough clue in itself.

Different rules seem to apply when there's a chance of fleecing the public out of their well-earned cash.

At the end of the day though, I held my hands up and paid the penalty, because let's face it, I had parked my car ten yards into the zone, which had obviously caused immense congestion, in and around London.

The truth is we can't seem to go anywhere now without the risk of being filmed and we seem to accept it with no opposition. This is because society has told us that cameras are needed for our own safety and protection.

We have now accepted the fact that it's perfectly fine for complete strangers to film our every move, but try and film your own daughter on a school sports day and you will immediately be stopped and told that it is not permitted where children are congregating, even though they will have dozens of CCTV cameras scattered all around the perimeter.

What next you may ask?

How about cameras in police helmets or lollipop ladies with a hidden camera in their lollipop?

Oh I forgot, that's happening already isn't it?

HAVING A YEARLY HIP CHECK

I went to have my eyes tested today and as I sat there trying to figure out which of the black circles in front of me were the clearest, I started to wonder just exactly why I was sitting there anyway.

The same thoughts came across me a couple of weeks ago, when I was lying in the dentist chair having my usual yearly dental check-up.

The good news today was there was no change in my eyes and as far as my teeth were concerned, they were all good as well, just like they were 12 months before and 12 months before that.

We don't have regular hip checks though do we, or regular knee checks or ankles? We just go whenever there is a problem, so why don't we do that with eyes and teeth?

Can you imagine going to the doctors every 12 months and asking to get your left elbow checked, even though it is fine and causing you no problem at all.

It's like calling in the plumber when you haven't got a leak, or reporting a gas leak when you can't smell gas. They'd just send you packing wouldn't they? So why are eyes and teeth treated differently to every other part of my anatomy?

I think that unless you're actually having a problem with them, then you're better off stopping at home.

Here's another thing... As I have got older, my hair has started to fall out. I haven't been to the doctors about it though, it's just happened over time. I haven't had regular yearly hair checks or even any help in maintaining what little hair I have... Unlike teeth.

"Your teeth are okay Mr Dorrance," the dentist will say, "but I think we'll just give them a little clean."

Can you imagine going the doctors about your hair?

"Your hair's okay Mr Dorrance, but I think I'll just run some V05 through it. Just pop your head in the bowl."

Sounds silly doesn't it, but what's the difference? He's just looking after the hair that I've got left... Just like the dentist does with my teeth.

Why all the fuss anyway? Teeth last for years! Even after we've left this mortal coil and our bodies are no more, your teeth will still carry on.

Only last week they uncovered a tooth that was 560,000 years old (apparently) and here we are, having yearly check-ups on ours.

We accept the fact that we need these regular dental and eye tests, because it's accepted as the 'norm', but everything else has to carry on regardless, until they start to pack up.

The thing is, if someone had brought in regular ankle tests a hundred years ago, then we would have merrily taken ourselves off to the ankle man every 12 months, without a care in the world wouldn't we? Regular ankle tests would now be taken as the 'norm', just like a dental or eye check is now, but it wasn't was it and that's why it sounds so ridiculous now?

What about a big toe check? It's getting sillier isn't it, but is it?

We have in-growing toenails, corns, verrucas, warts, fungal infections, athlete's foot, and a host of other things, all bubbling away under everyone's sock. But do we get a yearly toe check…? No chance. You'll have to wait, until it goes wrong I'm afraid.

DON'T BE FOOLED BY VALENTINE'S DAY

Every year on February the 14th millions of husbands are brainwashed into believing that flowers and chocolates are a must gift on Valentine's Day and are made to feel totally inadequate, if they dare fail to buy their loved one, that customary box of chocolates.

But forgetting to pick your wife's chocolates up on your way back from work, is not a crime and you shouldn't be made to feel guilty about it.

The blame for this ridiculous ritual, must be firmly laid at the feet of Richard Cadbury, because if it hadn't have been for that man introducing chocolate as a Valentine's gift idea in 1861, then you could have quite happily arrived home and got away with a quick smile and a cup of tea.

But it's not just Valentine's Day we have to contend with. There's a multitude of special days where cards, flowers and chocolates are expected.

They are not all in one month either are they? They are all strategically placed throughout the year. A clever plan to keep us all busy spending money.

Unfortunately, Valentine's Day comes at a time, when you're just getting over the awful effects of yet another hyped up frenzy... Christmas!

Yes, not only have you just had to tolerate the constant bombardment of cards, present buying, tinsel and mingling with people you don't usually like to mingle with, you now find yourself (in January) trying to do your weekly shop, while at the same time desperately trying to dodge the mass of Easter eggs, that have suddenly sprung up all around you.

Valentine's Day is the big pusher at this time though and there's no hope of escape, as everywhere you look there are reminders.

'Valentine's Day is nearly here' you will see draped across the supermarket entrance. 'Buy a box of chocolates', 'buy a bunch of flowers' and 'show your loved ones just how much you love them' is splashed across every aisle.

Now let's get one thing straight here...

Buying a box of chocolates, a bunch of flowers and a fancy card once a year, does not prove that you love someone.

Love is having a cup of tea together, love is having a laugh together, love is understanding each other, love is about being able to trust each other, love is knowing what love really is without spending a fortune on proving it. Love is all of those things, every day of the year and not just on February 14th.

As far as I'm concerned, Valentine's Day is not a romantic day at all. If anything, it has actually watered down true love. In fact out of any day of the year where love is at its weakest, you'll find that it'll be Valentine's Day. The love is cheap, even though you've probably spent a fortune on it.

Buying your love (which is exactly what it is) on one day of the year, has not been simpler either, with tips online suggesting just how your loved one can be wooed.

One tip suggests leaving a trail of rose petals on the floor leading them to the kitchen table, where a bottle of wine and a freshly cooked meal will be waiting.

Not only that, but it also recommends leaving a heart-shaped box of chocolates, some red and white teddy bears and some love hearts next to her dinner plate too.

To be honest... Anyone who falls for that type of carry on, doesn't deserve to be in a relationship anyway! It's false, it's plastic and it's anything but love.

Valentine's Day is just another day, devised to keep everyone busy doing nothing. Another money-making day that I refuse to get drawn into.

The 'You don't love me, because you didn't buy me anything' line, is a line that I no longer have to worry about anymore, because my wife knows that I don't need to buy her anything to show real love.

At the end of the day, Valentine's Day is just an easy way out for the masses. A quick nip to Sainsbury's for a card, a posh slab of chocolate, a cuddly toy and that's that! No real thought, just a robotic gesture.

So boycott Valentine's Day, because the more of you that accept it, the more of it will be thrown at you.

Bring back real love! Go and put the kettle on!

I'M NOT KILLING THE PLANET, HONEST

Apparently, if I don't start turning my standby button off on my DVD player, then the icecaps will melt, the ozone layer will vanish, the earth will evaporate and it's all going to happen within the next 50 years.

I have also been informed that the world will self-destruct if I keep leaving the tap running while cleaning my teeth.

I should also stop having a bath every night and only shower under a dribble, thus saving water and precious energy.

I have also been told that I should live in the dark as much as possible too!

Why though? Why should I suffer, when big business don't bother at all?

Why is it perfectly acceptable for Burger King to leave their fluorescent lights on 24-hours-a-day and for Pizza Hut to have their colossal sign flashing all night, but if I leave my kitchen light on for ten minutes, I am being selfish and wasting the world's resources.

As you know, we've had a dripping tap in the bathroom now for quite a while and although it will turn off, it will continue to drip, if you don't know the knack of turning it off properly.

My wife will occasionally point out to me that not only is this annoying, but it is also a complete waste of water.

I responded by reminding her of the water leak that occurred a few weeks ago in the next street, where thousands upon thousands of gallons of water gushed along the gutter for about two weeks.

I pointed out that our dripping tap would struggle to fill a saucepan in that time, so I very much doubt it would be adding to any long term water shortages at Severn Trent.

I do agree that we shouldn't be wasting energy. We should turn lights off when we don't need them, we should recycle whenever possible and we should definitely all do our bit to save the planet, but when you've got a McDonalds down the road lit up like the Starship Enterprise, then I don't really see why I should stumble around in the dark, fumbling around for my Sky remote standby button.

Nobody can accuse us of not doing our bit for the environment though. In fact I don't know anyone that recycles more than we do. We used to do recycling even before recycling was even invented. We don't waste anything in our house, not even the furniture.

We've got two sofas in the lounge. One of them we've had for over 30 years and the other one was my wife's granddad's. It must be at least 50 years old!

Occasionally we will buy a new throw-over for them and I do recall replacing two legs on one of them a few years ago, but apart from that, they've both been absolutely fine.

Now bear in mind that the average person will change their sofa approximately every five years. Taking that into account, this means we have saved the land fill at least 14 sofas since we've been married. Impressive or what?

But are we killing the planet anyway? Isn't all this global warming just a big myth?

Yes, we did have some terrible floods in Cumbria last year, but we've had floods and various other natural disasters before. For years in fact!

We had a Tsunami in 1607 and we had an earthquake in 1884, long before global warming or the hole in the ozone layer were even thought of.

We had the great storm of 1703 when over 4000 oaks were destroyed in the New Forest and at sea, shipwrecks killed a third of the navy.

The great frost of 1683–84 saw the Thames frozen solid to a depth of nearly two feet.

1816 was labelled 'the year without summer' when it rained constantly for 130 days. Global warming? I don't think so.

The world is just doing what it has always done. Over time, it changes, it adapts and me leaving my standby button on, or stumbling around in the dark, is not going to make a blind bit of difference…

I would just like to point out that since writing this, the dripping shower and taps have been fixed.

HAVING A WASH
SHOULD NOT BE A CHORE

Can someone please explain to me exactly what the pleasure is in taking a shower, because for the life of me, I cannot see any pleasure in it at all. I'm all for having a good wash obviously, but why stand up and do it?

Even then you can't wash all over because you're just standing in one place, so you have to move and move and keep on moving, which to me is ridiculous and something I don't find enjoyable at all.

Washing should be all about enjoyment, relaxing and contemplating. You shouldn't have to stand in a cold puddle, fumbling around for a bottle of shower gel or soap. What's the pleasure in that?

Washing the easy way is my philosophy and this is how you do it:

Fill the bath halfway up with lukewarm (verging on cold) water and then strip off and submerge yourself, until you are lying down and in a nice relaxed position.

Your head should be resting on the back of the bath and your feet should be within touching distance of the taps. This is very important, because the last thing you want to do is keep bending forwards turning the taps on and off, causing yourself unnecessary toil. At the end of the day, let your feet do the work. They are at that end of the bath anyway, so it makes more sense doesn't it?

It is very important to make sure the water is lukewarm or as cold as you can stand it at this point, because if it's not, you will not feel the benefits from the rest of your bathing experience.

It is also important to have your body wash nearby (reaching distance without having to bend) as you don't want to be getting out of the bath again. Not until you have finished bathing anyway.

Once you are happy and in position, relax and slowly lift your leg up and turn on the hot tap with your big toe. Then lower your leg, shut your eyes and wait…

Once the bath is full (and I mean full) turn off the tap (with your big toe) and relax even more.

All depending on how cold your water was in the first place, will depend on your overall bathing experience. Either way it will be still, wonderful and perfect.

One thing's for sure, after trying out this way of washing, you will find that taking a shower will almost certainly become a thing of the past.

If you think about it… It makes sense doesn't it?

You're having an all body wash, all at the same time AND you're lying down relaxing as well. How perfect is that?

I believe that whatever you do in life, however small; you need to make it as enjoyable, as comfortable and as easy as possible. Why make life hard for yourself?

My wife likes to take a shower. She feels that it's quick and easy and likes to be in and out, but to me that's just making it into a chore. A chore that needs to be done and as quickly as possible.

On the rare occasion that she does take a bath, she will lie in what can only be described as a puddle. She will lie in it for about five minutes, before turning over and wetting the other side.

To me this is just like having a shower, only in a horizontal position.

The way I see it is, if you're going to have a bath, then have a bloody bath!

The thing is, she does this because she likes to think that she's saving water, but why does she bother?

Only yesterday it was reported that 3,300,000,000 litres of water is being lost every day through leakage.

It was also reported that gardeners are using 220 gallons of water every single hour in the UK and that's just with their garden sprinklers, so I don't really think having a decent bath is going to make much of a difference do you? As far as I'm concerned, a bath is far more important to me, than Fred's lollipop garden in the next street.

It's all about making your life as enjoyable and as easy as possible and if that involves filling the bath up to the top (my way) with hot water and lots of bubbles, then so be it.

Unfortunately it is not always possible to wash the easy way though. Camping holidays are definitely one of those occasions.

The thought of traipsing across a field towards a cold shower block, with a toilet bag under one arm, a towel over the other, in a pair of flip flops, doesn't exactly fill me with the joys of spring. The simple fact is, there is no easy way to have a wash, while on a camping site and for this very reason, I avoid camping.

If for any reason I am unfortunate enough to find myself in a camping situation, then I find the best solution all round is to just not bother having a wash.

Strangely enough, there is a plus side to this.

If you're away for seven days, then at least your bathing experience will be seven times better when you return home AND it will be pure ecstasy, if you've been brave enough to stay away for a fortnight.

I'M NEVER ON MY OWN BECAUSE I'M WITH ME

Nobody should ever be lonely and deep down nobody really is and that's because you've got yourself.

When I'm out alone, I'm never on my own, because I'm with me.

I can quite easily keep myself company, I can talk things through, I can have a good laugh and If I'm miles from anywhere, I always know that I'll be okay, because I'm there too.

Always remember this, because it doesn't really matter how many friends you have in life, or how close you think your family is to you, the truth of the matter is, you're always on your own.

Most people think they've got best friends, but deep down they haven't, because the only best friend you've really got is you.

That's why you need to be aware of the world that is within you.

Knowing that you have this very special place of your own, keeps you strong and it keeps you safe. Nothing can hurt you, because you are in your world and not this one.

Knowing that you're okay on your own makes you a stronger person. That's because you don't have to depend on anyone else.

People can feel very lonely and that's because that inner self is missing.

This leads them to look for external things in life to make them happy and make them feel safe. They're looking for a crutch to lean on, but the problem with that is, that crutch can very often be taken away and when that happens, it brings them anxiety and loneliness.

Always remember, you don't need a crutch. You just need yourself, because there's nobody and nothing that is as strong as you are.

In A World On My own

When people rush about
It doesn't really matter to me
They can rush all they want
Because I'm somewhere else you see

I'm in my own little place
A place where nobody knows
It's somewhere very special
Somewhere, where nobody goes

So rush all you like
You worry, fret and moan
And I'll just carry on as normal
In a world on my own

HOW TO SURVIVE IN A SCUTTER TOWN

Scutter towns have sprung up all over the place in recent years. This has resulted in many people either stopping in their kennel whenever possible, or selling up and moving out to somewhere nice.

A good indication that your town is becoming a scutter town, is to look at the way people dress.

Don't be fooled by the odd well-dressed person walking about. They're probably just visiting, or just haven't managed to escape yet.

Another indication is to check out the towns hanging baskets (if they've got any).

One town I visited the other week, had a wonderful array of flowers. Every single hanging basket was bursting with colour. They were a joy to see.

The town I am currently standing in also have hanging baskets, but unfortunately these are bursting not with colour, but with dog ends, drinks cans and crisp packets.

So why erect empty hanging baskets in a town that obviously doesn't appreciate them?

Well, I can only presume that at some point in time, the council thought it was a good idea, tried it, but then decided to give it up as a lost cause. Something that obviously happens throughout the whole of the country. Yes, I'm afraid hanging baskets in scutter towns, have simply become hanging litter bins.

Spit, discarded chewing gum and dog mess on pavements, are other signs that you've entered a scutter town and trying to dodge around them, can be quite a skill in itself. In fact if dodging dog mess became an Olympic sport, then anyone living in a scutter town, I am sure, would be odds-on favourite to win a gold medal.

Another feat that is almost impossible to achieve, is trying to get from one end of the High Street to the other, without hearing the F word at least half a dozen times, as regrettably this has become part of the scutter town language.

So what can be done to escape scutter towns?

Well, the obvious solution is to up sticks and clear off to somewhere nice. Unfortunately, many people haven't got the money to do this, which means you very often find yourself having to make do with what you've got, until the time arises, when you can finally uproot and escape for good.

The good news is, there are things that you can do to make life easier, while planning your escape.

Try and surround yourself with likeminded people. People who are also looking at escaping Scutterville and have the same goals as you.

When you find yourself in crowded places, bring up the drawbridge and retreat to your special place.

Try to use self-service machines as much as possible, such as supermarkets and banks. Doing this will reduce the risk of coming into contact with scutter town inhabitants. The more you can minimise the risk of that, the easier life will be for you.

As the main weekly shop is concerned, choose your supermarket wisely.

Visit a few first and try and gauge what type of shoppers shop there. Once you are happy, try and stick to that one, but always remembering to bring the drawbridge up whenever you feel the need to do so.

Don't get involved in scutter town projects either. You will always find some dedicated group, that is totally committed in organising events for the town, but unfortunately they usually consist of just four or five people, and although a bake the cupcake competition at the local scutter town fete, followed by a raffle to win a naff teddy bear, might go some way in helping, it's not really going to change the fact that the town is still a dump and that no one else really cares.

You will also realise that fundraising to make your scutter town a better place, is not really worth all the hassle, when you discover that the memorial bench your local group donated to the park a few months earlier, has since been vandalised with graffiti and used chewing gum.

The trouble is, once your town has become a scutter town, it is very difficult to change it back again, so you should seriously think about escaping as soon as possible.

If on the other hand, you feel quite happy living amongst the dog mess, the bad language and crisp packet hanging baskets, then carry on as normal and just pretend I haven't said anything.

TRYING TO WORK OUT THE BEST WAY TO CLEAN MY TEETH

Popping out to buy a tube of toothpaste sounds like a simple enough task doesn't it? But have you ever stood in the shopping aisle and tried to figure out which one to buy?

One company have got a toothpaste called 'Total Care', but if it's total care, why do they sell dozens of other types as well? If it's 'Total Care', don't you just need the one?

To me it means just that, but no! The shelves are full of alternatives. Repair and Protect, Repair and Protect Extra Fresh, Repair and Protect Whitening, Complete Protection, Extra Whitening, Tartar Control, Fresh Impact, Pronamel and that's just a few. There are hundreds more, all claiming to do something different, even though we are sold 'Total Care'.

Let's take a look at the sensitive toothpastes.

There's a standard sensitive toothpaste, but there's also a sensitive repair toothpaste as well.

The thing is, why do we need the sensitive toothpaste, if the other one repairs them as well?

It's like having a slow puncture in your tyre and you keep blowing it up, instead of fixing the hole.

At the end of the day, surely you just need the one toothpaste? A total care toothpaste that does just that? It will clean them, protect the enamel and repair any sensitivity!

Obviously if you want to look like some Hollywood celeb with huge plastic white choppers, then that's a completely different issue, but as far as the day to day care of your teeth go, a one only total care toothpaste, is surely all we need.

There are many other brands of products out there, that like toothpaste bring much confusion.

Headache tablets are a perfect example.

GlaxoSmithKline are the manufacturers of Panadol. Panadol is a good tablet when faced with an headache, but instead of taking the ordinary standard Panadol tablets, why not take the Panadol Advance tablets? They're faster acting or maybe Panadol Extra or why not Panadol Actifast?

Hang on a bit though… If you're in pain, then surely you want the pain to go away as quickly as possible anyway don't you, so why even bother with the ordinary standard Panadol?

In fact what's the point in even making it?

Surely we just need the one tablet, the one tablet that is going to kill the pain fast?

It's like going to the dentist with an aching tooth and the dentist saying.

"I'm afraid you need a filling Mr Dorrance. I can numb your gum, but you will be in pain for at least 20 minutes. Is that okay, or do you want me to numb it properly?"

They also manufacture Panadol Night. This is a drowsy version to make you sleep, but sleeping isn't the problem is it? You just want to remove the pain. Buying something that only works when you're lying in bed is ridiculous!

Like toothpaste, there are too many variations. Too many, all doing the same job.

What about this for an idea?

How about an Anadin Extra toothpaste? Give them time, I'm sure it will happen

IS IT A TRAIN STATION OR THE STARSHIP ENTERPRISE?

For the last few weeks, everyone has been raving about New Street Station in Birmingham, which has been redeveloped at a cost of £750 million pounds.

To be honest though, I couldn't really see what was wrong with it in the first place. You could walk about with ease, pick up a magazine or a book, have a nice relaxing coffee while waiting for your train and it also had the biggest information board in the world... In fact it was perfect.

Unfortunately that has now all gone and instead, has been replaced with what can only be described as a very large Matalan, with lights so bright, sunglasses have become a necessity.

Yes, the days of sitting and having a relaxing cup of coffee are well and truly over, as you now find yourself supping your frothy cappuccino, amongst thousands of frenzied shoppers and commuters, as they all frantically dash about, as if they've been on speed for about six months.

The building itself has become a world of bright lights, noise and zig-zag architecture. The straight walls now slant to the left, the pillars slant to the right, the flat ceiling bends up and down and the floor is bright, curved and nobbly.

Unfortunately my local town's train station is also in the process of having a makeover, which means the transformation to the Starship Enterprise, complete with chaos, flashing lights and at a cost of millions (even though it's perfectly okay the way it is already, apart from the odd dumb us down sign), is well and truly on the cards.

The problem is, all new developments are going the same way. Designers seem to be living in some kind of gaming world. A gaming world that they've allowed to cross over into this one.

You enter any new shopping centre development and you'll soon start to wonder if you are in a shopping centre, or whether you've actually been transported into some level of Ratchet & Clank.

Parking can be a problem too, as the lead up to the entrance is most certainly designed NOT to help, but confuse. The designer had obviously got his inspiration from playing Mario Kart.

Once in the car park, the confusion continues, as you are then confronted with various bends, arrows and ramps, all slanting off in weird, confusing directions. Around the clock playing on his Nintendo had certainly paid off.

My father-in-law and mother-in-law got really confused the other week while visiting one of these places. It took them almost an hour to park the car and following a quick shop around Primark, took them another hour to find it again. They have since vowed never to go back, and to be honest I'm not surprised.

Everything was just too much for them, such as number plate recognition, confusing road layouts, slanted car park spacing and hidden-away ramps etc.

It's all very well if you're a dab hand at computer gaming, but as they are both 86, they were finding it all a little bit more complicated than most.

At the end of the day, we just want to park the car. We want it to be as easy and as straightforward as possible. We don't need any bright spark trying to impress us, with fancy confusing layouts.

Just keep it simple Mr Designer, because if you do that, everybody will be happy. You also won't have 86 year olds wandering about shopping centre's in a state of bewilderment.

If on the other hand you quite like the sound of your mother-in-law stumbling around, baffled and in a state of shock, then I can't think anywhere better than New Street Station to do it.

I promise you, drop her off there and you won't see her for weeks.

BUY NOW AND PAY LATER?

A few years ago I had a bill off British Telecom, asking me to pay £68.42 for their unlimited call package.

It really was a fantastic deal. You could call anyone, at any time of the day, seven days a week. Sounds good doesn't it?

The problem was, I wasn't with British Telecom, I was with AOL.

As this was the case, I decided to call the British Telecom customer services helpline.

Unfortunately I soon found myself being diverted 2000 miles to a remote village somewhere on the outskirts of Bangladesh.

After about ten minutes of us trying to understand each other, Ashik on the other end of the line, finally came to the conclusion that it had been a mistake and that I had been overcharged.

It turns out that I should have only been charged for the line rental of £34.50 I was told not to worry though, as the over charge would be credited on my next quarterly bill. This started me thinking.

If you went into an hairdresser and you were charged £20 for an haircut, you wouldn't be expected to pay £40 and then have to wait three months to get £20 back would you?

If you employed a window cleaner and you were charged £15 to have you windows cleaned, you wouldn't be expected to pay £30 and then wait three months to get £15 back would you?

If you went into a restaurant and you were charged £15 for a meal, you wouldn't be expected to pay £30 and then have to wait three months to get £15 back either would you? So why was British Telecom any different?

I know someone who volunteers to pay his telephone bill 12 months up front! Twelve months up front!!!

He also has to make sure there's a direct debit set up, just so's they can take out any additional monthly charges... Oh and not only that, he has to sign up for paper-free billing as well.

Basically, they want his money up front, total control of his bank account and not be inconvenienced by sending him out any bills.

All this for a measly 10% discount.

What's that going to get him? A loaf of bread? A tub of Clover? Half a dozen eggs? Not worth it is it?

Why put himself through all that hassle and pay up front for the privilege? Why not just haggle for the best deal and keep his money in his bank account?

Too many companies are doing this now. Not satisfied with forcefully emptying your bank account every month, they want most of it up front as well.

Basically you're paying for a service that you haven't even used yet.

Imagine going into Tesco and paying for a bag of crisps that you're not going to eat?

"A bag of crisps please"

"That will be 54p."

"No problem. Here's the money, I'll come back in six months and pick them up"

The chances are, you'll probably change your mind by then anyway.

GOING TO THE DOCTORS, BUT ONLY IF YOU KNOW WHAT'S WRONG WITH YOU

I recently had a bit of a tight chest, which was also aching slightly. I had a lump in my throat too and was finding it a little bit difficult to swallow, so I thought I'd take myself off to the doctors and get it checked out

So what happened?

Well, he had a quick listen to my chest, gazed at me for about a minute, looked at his computer for a few seconds and that was about it. The truth of the matter was, he hadn't got a clue. He just sat there in silence, completely baffled.

I decided to break the silence.

"Do you think it may be a chest infection?" I said, as I could see he was really struggling

"It could be," was his reply, as he looked at his computer screen yet again.

This was followed by yet another few minutes of awkwardness, as his brain continued to tick over (I could hear it).

To be fair, most doctors I've seen do struggle to some extent, but this one was failing miserably on all counts.

What gets me is he could have asked me a multitude of questions, but he asked me nothing.

Why didn't he ask me about my diet?

As far as he was concerned, I could be drinking 30 pints of lager a day and living on chips and crisps, but he wouldn't know would he, because he didn't ask. I could be having a fried breakfast every morning cooked in duck fat, followed by a Cadbury's Cream Egg and a bottle of wine.

I could be snacking throughout the day on Monster Munch, tubs of Pringles and drinking goose blood by the bucket load. I could be knocking back a bottle of whiskey every afternoon, half a dozen donuts and four glasses of port couldn't I? If I was doing all these things and he knew that I was, then maybe he'd have been able to say, "No wonder you've got a tight chest Mr Dorrance, maybe you should consider changing your diet?" But he had no idea, hence the gormless look.

I've slowly come to the conclusion over the years, that it's actually no good going to see your GP, unless you know exactly what's wrong with you in the first place.

The secret is to find out the problem before you go. If you can do that, then you're onto a winner.

Anyway, you'll be glad to know I didn't bother with the antibiotics that he finally decided to give me and within a few days, I was as right as rain again.

To be honest, I try not to go to the doctors at all if I can help it. I think it's best to stay away if you can, because not only do they not know what they are doing most of the time, but they also tend to treat you for something that you didn't even go about.

Head off to the Doctors with a frozen shoulder and you could soon find yourself on 2 mg of Ramipril, by the time you come out.

Yes, just one blip in your blood pressure reading and you could find yourself just one step away from the hypertension register. Once that happens, I'm afraid your trip to the doctors will never be the same again, as you'll find your blood pressure will be checked on every single visit.

This means that there will be no safe haven for you anymore, as even a simple boil on your backside will require a blood pressure check. This will ultimately result in the Doctor upping your Ramipril to 4 mg without even a mention of the swelling on your left cheek.

Making appointments can be a bit of a nightmare too, especially if you've got more than one thing wrong with you.

Wake up with a dodgy head and a pain in your knee and you'll have to decide which one you think is more important, as you'll only be able to make an appointment for either one or the other.

"You'll have to make two appointments, if you want to see him about both," the receptionist will say, as you struggle to make a decision.

The big question is, do you carry on with the headache, or do you sort out your limp?

Sometimes you'll book an appointment for one thing, only to find that you've got something else wrong with you by the time you get there.

"I've got an appointment for my head, but I hurt my arm this morning," you will say on your arrival.

"I'm sorry Mr Dorrance, but we're fully booked at the moment," she'll say. "I can always book your arm in for next week though?"

Another trait that doctors seem to struggle with is handwriting. For some reason, writing properly is beyond any doctors capabilities and a scribble is usually about as much as you can hope for.

This was never a problem for my doctor that I used to go and see a few years ago though, as he didn't bother with writing at all. Doctor Singh used to draw pictures instead.

I remember going to see him with what looked like the possible signs of an umbilical hernia. I walked in, sat down and explained my symptoms.

Following a quick examination, he decided to refer me to a specialist. He reached for a piece of paper and instead of scribbling down the details, decided to draw a picture of my belly button instead.

"Give this to the receptionist," he said, "she will arrange your appointment".

Sure enough, I headed out to the reception area and handed the piece of paper to Sheila the receptionist.

"Doctor Singh wants you to make an appointment for me," I said, as I pointed to the belly button drawing.

"Just take a seat Mr. Dorrance and I'll get that arranged," she said, as she picked up the telephone.

I headed over to the waiting area and sat down. Suddenly, I heard a shout.

"Mr Dorrance?"

I looked around and there stood Sheila, holding the piece of paper in the air.

"Is it the eye specialist you've got to see?" she said, with a vague look on her face.

"No, that's my belly button that is!" I replied back

"Oh, It's just that Mr. Singh has drawn an eye on here?" she said, as she turned the paper around to see if it made any difference.

"No, it's definitely my belly button!" I replied, as people around me, tried desperately not to laugh.

"Okay," she said, sounding like she was clearly not convinced. "I'll just double check with the doctor"

But why was she checking with him? I'm the one with the ailment and I know where my belly button is. Just because he couldn't draw properly, I had to sit and wait and get approval.

I couldn't help but wonder what would have happened, if I hadn't have waited and intervened? What if I'd have just gone home and left it to the 'professionals to sort out'? I had visions of turning up at the eye specialist a few weeks later, stripping off to the waist and directing my belly button at him.

What if I'd have come out the doctors with a prescription? Showing off my belly button would have been embarrassing enough, but trying to explain why I had also been squirting Optrex in it for the past six weeks, would have been even more so.

You should always have your wits about you when the medical profession are around. Keeping away is the obvious choice for me though, because the slightest thing can very often lead to something else.

My friend went to the doctors with a splinter in his finger and ended up having a prostate examination. A splinter that could have quite easily been dealt with at home, but felt the need to go to the doctors with it.

So how did he get on? Well the good news is, the splinter was successfully removed and his finger is back on the mend.

All he's got to do now is sit tight and wait for his PSA results to come back.

HE CAN RIDE A BIKE, GIVE HIM A GONG

Yesterday we had yet more floods throughout the UK. This resulted in thousands of people being displaced from their homes.

We also had a terrorist attack in Iraq, which resulted in over 80 people being killed.

With all this going on around the world, you would have thought that Barbara Windsor becoming a Dame, would have been way down in the packing order of news wouldn't you, but no, it turns out Babs was way more important than anything else that was going on and this was apparent, as her fizz hog was overwhelmingly splashed right across every news bulletin and newspaper going.

Another 'celeb' in the New Year's honours list also got major coverage, picking up an OBE for reading the news.

Knighthoods were also dished out to a rugby player, two footballers, a jockey and Damon Albarn who once sang a song about life in parks.

Meanwhile an athlete who rides a bike got an OBE for services to sport. An actor got an MBE for services to acting and on it goes. I didn't see an engineer from Virgin Media get anything for services for his broadband installation skills though… But what's the difference?

At the end of the day, they're all just doing a job and as far as I'm concerned, just doing a job shouldn't lead to receiving a gong.

Another thing... A Virgin Media engineer will not start his career with a nice little lottery grant will he? And he certainly won't end up on the Santander advert earning a fortune, just because he's become the UK's best broadband installer. All the best a Virgin Media engineer can hope for is either an extra few days holiday a year, or maybe a new van every two.

So what about lottery funding then and how come you can apply for it if you run round a track, but you can't if you want to install broadband for a living? Well the simple answer is... I have no idea.

To me, there isn't any difference. They are both careers, except the Virgin Media engineer doesn't get a leg up... Unlike the runner.

The funding goes up over time too.

Athletes on the highest level of grants get almost £28,000 per year and that doesn't include all the coaching, physiotherapy and medical support.

Then at some point in the future, if they do manage to win medals, they are treated like heroes and ultimately given a godlike status.

On their journey to success, they are praised to the hilt by the media. An inspiration to us all, they've won gold for Great Britain and they've worked so hard to bring us more golds than ever before.

They haven't done it for us though have they? They haven't done it for me.

Let's put this in perspective.

The only reason they've done it, is because they've wanted to do it. They've wanted that medal and they've done it for no one else but themselves. You certainly don't see them giving them away do you?

They've done very well in a career that we've funded! A funded career that results in million pound advertising deals.

I had a look at the Lottery website today and they are extremely proud of their achievements too

Thank you! Every time you play the National Lottery, you help support British sport.

National Lottery funding pays for elite athletes to train full time and have access to some of the best coaching and facilities in the world.

I cannot think of any other profession, where you would receive this kind of help to follow your career path.

Imagine asking for lottery funds for starting up a window cleaning round, or wanting to be a plumber or long distance lorry driver OR even a Virgin Media broadband installer. It just wouldn't happen would it? But why not? They are all careers. I'm afraid you would have to struggle on and sort it out for yourself. You've decided to be a postman, so you're stuck with it.

Here's a thought though for anyone out there that hasn't had a £28,000-a-year lottery grant.

Next time you see some Olympian on TV trying to sell you a bank account, just think about the life you could have had, if only you'd have run around a track instead.

GET YOURSELVES A BAR OF PHARMACOLOGICAL ACTIVITY

Have you ever had one of those coughs that just won't stop? The type of cough, that keeps you awake all night long?

Well don't worry, because finally at last, researchers have come to the conclusion that I was right all along.

There's been a report out recently that says the best cure for a cough is chocolate.

I've been saying this for years! Forget the honey and lemon, or sucking a Locket… Get some chocolate down your neck.

The report went on to say that the reason chocolate is good for coughs, is because of the demulcent properties of cocoa. It has a pharmacological activity, which has some sort of inhibitory effect on the nerve endings themselves… Basically it puts a coating on your throat.

I always remember when my daughter was about three years old. She was lying in bed desperately trying to get to sleep, but couldn't because she'd got such a terrible cough. It just wouldn't go away, which meant she was getting really frustrated and upset.

'A packet of Chocolate Buttons will do the trick,' I thought and sure enough, after just one, she was cough free and off to sleep she went.

The thing is, even though this recent report has come out and we now have the evidence, the medical profession will still continue to take you down the cough medicines and cough sweets route.

I dare you to take a trip down to your local pharmacy and ask them what they recommend for a cough. I bet you won't come out with a bar of Dairy Milk or a Cadbury's Twirl? It will be a bottle of cough medicine, even though there is little, or any proof that it will actually help you at all.

As I have mentioned before, chocolate can be very useful. Not only can it save your life when driving, but you now know it will help you sleep when coughing. In other words, it helps you stay awake AND it also helps you nap... How clever is that?

We do have to be very careful and not get too carried away though. Just because I have highlighted a couple of chocolate benefits, I am not suggesting you all go out and stock up on Mint Aero's. Just the opposite... You should only eat chocolate when it is absolutely necessary.

So what about other chocolate 'benefits' that have been claimed by the so-called 'experts'? Well, apparently chocolate helps lift depression. I can see the reasoning behind that, however I am also aware that eating chocolate puts on weight and brings you out in spots, so I'm guessing within a fortnight, you'll probably be twice as depressed as you were in the first place.

I've also read that chocolate has anti-aging effects. It slows down the aging process... Really? I'm afraid I'd have to disagree.

I know a 46-year-old woman who eats a slab of chocolate at least every day and has done so all her life.

Unfortunately, this woman now resembles a 96-year-old, she's got skin like a dishevelled prune and hobbles around like an old donkey with athlete's foot, so you can safely say it hasn't worked for her. Anybody who thinks sucking on a Twix every day will bring eternal youth, should seriously think again.

Apparently, eating chocolate can also help greatly with your digestive system. This is of course nonsense.

Chocolate is a clogger! Especially when you've been indulging in other foods as well, like bread and cheese for instance.

In other words, eat a cheese sandwich and a Toffee Crisp and suddenly you'll find you've entered the world of 'goo and glue food'. Too much of that caper and you'll find that a colon irrigation session could be just around the corner. So unless you want gallons of water shot up your rectum, I suggest you seriously think about whether you really should be eating that Cadbury's Flake and a cheese and onion cob.

As I say, chocolate should be for emergencies only. It should not be part of your daily diet. You'll get fat, you will be depressed, you will get spots, you will look old and you will clog your colon up!

On the upside though, at least you'll sort that cough out.

THE BEST WAY TO LOOK AFTER YOUR GUTS

I decided recently that I wanted to send some friendly bacteria down into my gut and so instead of buying a pack of those puny milky yoghurt tubs from the Asda, thought that it would be a good idea to buy a bottle of friendly bacteria capsules instead.

There were lots to choose from.

One bottle claimed to contain millions of organisms, with another bottle claiming to contain billions of organisms. Others were labelled up at one billion, two billion, three billion, four billion, eight billion, ten billion and even fourteen billion.

Eventually I stumbled across what seemed to be the king of all probiotic capsules. I went for the Ultra Maximum Acidophilus capsules, with a staggering 20 billion friendly bacteria inside.

It was one hell of a claim, but never the less I bought them anyway and have been taking one a day, for the past week.

When I pop a capsule in though, how do I know that there are 20 billion of them in there? Who's counted them?

It's not as if I'm taking a magnesium and vitamin B6 tablet is it, or a calcium and vitamin D tablet, or even a multivitamin, which claim to contain up to 35 vitamins? This one's got 20 billion!

Not only that, but it says 20 billion friendly bacteria guaranteed!!!

If you look closely at the label though, at the bottom of the bottle in small print, it reads: *20 billion friendly bacteria guaranteed 'at the time of manufacture'*.

This has obviously been put on to cover themselves against any comebacks.

What do they think I'm going to do though? Sit up in bed all night and count them? I'm not exactly going to say

"I'm sorry, but there's two short" am I?

All I know is there were 60 capsules when I started and now there's 53.

So what about those little pots of probiotic yogurts? Some claim to contain between 8-10 billion strains of friendly bacteria.

The trouble is, they also contain two teaspoons of sugar as well and if that isn't bad enough, they also contain maltodextrin, which also turns to sugar once in the body, so all in all you're probably better off sucking on a Galaxy Ripple instead...

I was interested to see if you could also get probiotics for pets too, and you won't be surprised to learn that you can.

Usually, all your dog's got to look forward to is his bowl of Pedigree Chum and a dog biscuit, but now he can look after his gut just like you.

Yes, you'll be glad to know the market is now littered with doggy probiotic supplements.

For as little as £20 per month, you can get a dog probiotic with 58 billion friendly bacteria in it... 58 billion!!! Your dog won't know what's hit it.

Apparently (according to the 'experts') dogs can experience digestive problems and taking probiotics can be very beneficial.

Maybe if your dog didn't eat bowls of offal, lips, eyeballs and god knows what else though, then maybe he wouldn't get digestive problems in the first place.

But what if you've got a different type of pet?

Well there's no need to worry there either, because probiotics are also available for cats, rabbits, chipmunks, hamsters, ferrets, gerbils, guinea pigs, mice, rats and even goldfish. In fact whatever the pet, there's a probiotic supplement for it.

Our goldfish has never had a probiotic in his life though, and he's been just fine. He's never had any conditioner added to his water either. Conditioner is to neutralise harmful metals and chlorine, which the 'professionals' state can be lethal to goldfish!

This is of course complete nonsense, as our goldfish has survived for over 20 years, on nothing more than a pinch of food and a tank full of Severn Trent. Not one single probiotic and water straight from the tap

With this in mind, I have taken the following steps.

I've thrown away the probiotics and replaced them with a light breakfast and a glass of tap water... Well, if it's good enough for the goldfish, then it's good enough for me.

WHAT'S NOT ON TELEVISION TONIGHT?

As I'm sitting here writing this book, most of the country are sitting in front of a TV watching a man dressed in a bunny outfit, trying to get foam carrots into a blue bucket.

This type of programme dumbs down millions of people every day. They even Sky Plus it, just in case they are late back from Matalan, but does it really matter if you miss the man in a bunny suit?

Television is very powerful, it is the focal point of family life and manipulates and controls the population. Even when there is nothing to watch, it still gets left on and people stare at it for hours.

A few months ago, I went to visit an old friend and as we sat in the lounge talking about old times, I realised that there were five of us in the room. There was myself, my wife, my friend, his wife and the 72-inch flat screen television that was mounted on the wall.

There was a rugby match on, but the strange thing is, nobody was actually watching it, it was just burning away at the electricity supply.

At some point my friend asked me what my thoughts on rugby were. I pointed out that I hated it, found it totally boring and would rather put my head through a mangle than watch it all afternoon. He said that he wasn't too fussed about it either, but that didn't deter him, he still left it on.

The weird thing is, even though I do detest rugby, I still couldn't stop myself from taking the occasional glance at the screen. The problem is, televisions are like magnets, you get drawn into them, no matter what crap is on.

Most people will tell you that television is rubbish and that there is never anything on worth watching, but drive up any street in the land and you will find the whole family glued to a television set, as if their life depended on it.

The biggest draw by far in television are soaps. We just can't get enough of them, can we?

So how will the latest love triangle unfold in your favourite soap?

Probably the same way as it unfolded in the previous love triangle last year, which incidentally was the same storyline, just with different actors.

At least when you watch a film, the film does actually end, unlike a soap. Soaps do not have endings, they are just on a continuous loop. A soap is something that you will watch for the rest of your life, yet you will never get to see the ending!

Then you turn over and it's that bloke again. The bloke who presented a programme last night... Oh and he was presenting another programme the night before that AND he's on daytime TV with some smiley woman.

Anyway, he's on again... Thirty minutes of exaggerated smiles, an overexcited studio audience, a comedian who isn't very funny and a 'celeb' who became famous last year, for singing really badly, on a show that was presented by the very same presenter.

These shows are supposed to 'entertain' us, but instead, they just exist. They dumb us down and instead of 'entertaining', they just keep our minds inactive. This means we are permanently planted to our sofa's and robotised into thinking that we are actually enjoying ourselves. We will be laughing at things that are not remotely funny, we will be believing things that are dangerously untrue and we will be staring at things for hours on end, with no idea why we're staring at them.

Reach for the off button. It will reenergise your mind, it will help you free your creativity and it will allow you to create new worlds, instead of being bogged down in this plastic robotic one.

ANIMALS DON'T NEED CHEMISTS DO THEY?

Isn't it weird how most humans need tablets and potions to get through life, yet a sparrow, a blackbird or any other animal for that matter, can get through it quite easily, without anything?

In fact, what do sparrows do when they get a headache? They certainly don't reach for the paracetamol do they? And what if a seagull gets an upset stomach? I can't really imagine it sucking on an antacid tablet can you?

Nature seems to be able to get on just fine without it all, but humans can't seem to survive without some kind of drug or medical aid.

On a recent visit to a quaint little village in Buckinghamshire, I sat by a duck pond and watched as the ducks idled their afternoon in the sunshine.

There were at least 40 ducks there, some swimming, some walking about and some having a doze. They all looked very content and relaxed.

After a while others joined them and it wasn't too long, before the whole area was covered with snoozing ducks.

The thing is, there wasn't any of them that looked like they were in pain… Not one had its wing up holding its head, or throwing up in the pond. They all looked absolutely fine, yet on the two benches opposite, four out of seven humans were ill.

Two had got an headache, one was complaining about his stomach and another was taking his blood pressure tablets. Now have you ever known a duck with high blood pressure? No me neither.

Then suddenly, another human turned up, sat down and proceeded to cough.

Over on the pond meanwhile, two swans majestically paddled over to settle down amongst the water lilies.

Suddenly the man with the high blood pressure stood up and headed off towards the chip shop. He was quite big and was puffing on a cigarette.

The coughing human meanwhile, was rummaging through her handbag, frantically searching for something (a cough lozenge I presume).

The man opposite holding his stomach, was fumbling around in his inside jacket pocket and because he was letting out a sporadic painful whimper, I gathered that he must have been searching around for his Rennies.

Unlike humans, animals don't need Rennies. Animals just let nature sort things out. They certainly don't need anything from the chemist.

Meanwhile the two headache patients on the other bench were definitely a bit worse for wear, as they were now both bent over groaning, one with his head in his hands.

I suppose nobody really knows if animals do get headaches, but I'm guessing if there's going to be one that does, then I would have thought the main contender would have to be the woodpecker.

Woodpeckers hammer their heads into trees with a force of 15 mph at 20 times a second. That's some going isn't it? Now if that's not going to give you a headache, then I don't know what will.

It doesn't seem to bother them though does it? You check a woodpecker out after a 20 minute hammering session and they'll cheerfully fly off and carry on with their day.

Following my couple of hours by the pond, I decided to say farewell to the ducks, the swans and the decrepit human beings that had congregated around it and head off into the village.

On my way I noticed half a dozen rabbits running around the field. One of them seemed to have a bit of a limp. It didn't seem to bother him though.

A human would have headed straight off to the doctors, who would have then handed him a prescription for either a knee support, some pain killers, or both.

I can't really imagine a rabbit in a Tubigrip though can you? Not only would it look pretty stupid, but like the rest of the animal world, he wouldn't need one anyway, because as I say, they just get on with it.

Suddenly, sure enough, that's exactly what this rabbit did. He ran across the field, through an hedge and out of sight.

WHY PLASTER WRAPPERS ARE LIFE THREATENING

I cut my finger the other day and because it was bleeding so much, I did what any intelligent person would do. I headed straight for the first aid box.

Once I'd finally managed to get the lid off, I seemed to find myself in a very worrying, life-threatening situation… I was desperately trying to get the plaster out of its packet, before bleeding to death.

Who the hell designs the packaging? Surely there's somebody out there, that can design a quick release plaster?

So what happened?

Well, the first thing I had to do, was try and separate the plaster from the rest of the strip.

This was quite an easy operation, as each plaster has got a perforated edge, but getting the plaster out of its individual packet was a complete nightmare. It just didn't want to come out!

Luckily, I managed to separate the edge of the packet, release the plaster and get it on my finger, before a blood transfusion was necessary.

This led me to delve deeper into the world of plasters and you won't be surprised to learn, that it's a world that is full of choice.

We've got wash-proof plasters, clear plasters, tough waterproof fabric plasters, we've even got Postman Pat and Peppa Pig plasters, but unless you're a dab hand at opening them, you're going to struggle big time AND bleed quite a lot.

Surely a quick release plaster is a pretty obvious solution. You press a button, the plaster pops up, you pull it, the backing comes off and you put it on your finger. Why hasn't this been invented?

Nearly one hundred years after the first plaster was introduced and here we are, still fumbling around, trying to get the damn thing out.

Don't worry though, because apparently there's some gel on the way. This means that we'll be able to do away with plasters altogether.

Yes, this revolutionary new gel stops bleeding immediately, which means that plasters could be a thing of the past.

They reckon that it works with the body's healing mechanisms to clot blood and then the bleeding stops.

This is all very well, but I can guarantee that this new wonder gel will have a child proof lid, a lid that will almost be impossible to get off.

This will be made even worse by the fact that you'll be squirting blood all over the kitchen floor, which means you'll soon be wishing that those dreaded plasters, had never gone away in the first place.

Trying to fish a plaster out of its packet is hard enough, but it's even worse in our house, because the trouble is, you've got to find the plasters in the first place.

My wife has a tendency to put plasters in a place where no one would ever dream of looking.

If I do manage to find them and put them back where they are supposed to be (i.e. the first aid box), I can guarantee that within a few hours, that box will be hidden away, at the back of the wall cabinet, behind a mountain of other bottles, containers and a yoghurt maker.

This means that trying to recover a plaster in an emergency, will very often result in most of the cabinet contents ending up in the sink. This is KerPlunk while bleeding to death, folks.

Finally, if you're lucky and the box has been recovered successfully, there's a huge possibility that the pack of plasters have been removed anyway.

If this is the case, then you may as well abandon the search and call for an ambulance, because the chances of finding them is very remote. In fact, they could be anywhere.

At the end of the day, plasters are a good invention, once you manage to get one out and onto your injury, but to me the invention is only half complete.

It's like how tins of beans used to be. A tin full of beans, but no way of getting into them without a tin opener. Luckily, over the last few years, the tin of beans invention has finally been completed, with the introduction of peel back lids.

This is how I feel about plasters. A great invention, but an invention, that was never quite accomplished.

DON'T TALK PEOPLE'S HEADS OFF

I very much believe that people who say a lot, usually have very little to say and people with a lot to say, usually say very little... True isn't it?

There's nothing worse than having to listen to endless, pointless wittering by someone who rabbles on for hours, when most things in life can be said in just one sentence.

If your car has just had an MOT and it needed two new tyres, then your car has just had an MOT and it needed two new tyres. We don't really need to know all the ins and outs of what time the garage opened, or that you were going to change them in the week, but you couldn't because a friend of your Auntie Barbara was due to go on holiday AND because she couldn't get to the airport, you had to take her to the blah blah blah blah blah blah blah.

What you must remember is, if you're the one that is telling the story, then it may sound extremely interesting and relevant to you, but I assure you it won't to your poor listener. They will have switched off and already started planning their escape route, way before you've even reached the Auntie Barbara bit.

You can also be assured that your listener will do their utmost to avoid you in the future, such as walking on the opposite side of the street, diverting your calls to answer phone, or will always be in a rush to get somewhere, if ever they accidently bump into you.

Boring the pants off people with long, mundane, uninteresting stories is one thing, but being an 'over chatty know all' is another.

I always think that it's best to just keep your mouth shut if for any reason you are not quite sure about something, but an 'over chatty know all' will not do this, because they ARE sure about absolutely everything. You name it, they know it, they've done it and by George they will make sure they tell you about it as well.

I was unfortunate enough to bump into an 'over chatty know all' a few weeks ago and because there was no escape (it was in a waiting room) I was trapped and forced to engage in a conversation.

The trouble was we'd never met before, so I didn't realise he was an 'over chatty know all' until he replied to my 'Are you from Ross-on-Wye?' question. This was a question that I wished I'd never asked.

Over the next twenty minutes, I was given a full in depth history of the town, the best place to park, the best pub to drink in, the best chip shop; the nearest cash point and the best bed and breakfast. He was just full of local area knowledge.

"If I was you I wouldn't go there, if you want my advice I'd eat here," etc. etc. etc. AND guess what? He wasn't actually from Ross-on-Wye, he was from Swansea!

Someone else in the room made the grave mistake of mentioning that they wanted to buy a motor home and guess what? He knew the best one to buy, where to get the best deal and YES... He'd had four different types and he'd been all over Europe in them.

Another person mentioned that they were thinking about buying a caravan and asked him if he'd ever had one. If that wasn't bad enough, they then asked him if he had any advice?

My jaw dropped... I couldn't believe what I'd just heard. Obviously he'd had one and of course he had plenty of advice.

Luckily my name was called and I managed to escape the onslaught.

It goes without saying that these types of people should be avoided at all costs, and that's exactly what I 'try' to do.

Sometimes this is unavoidable though, which means that if you are unfortunate to bump into one, you will have to carefully plan your escape route as soon as possible.

Pretending your name has been called is just one of them... It worked for me anyway.

APPRECIATE WHAT YOU ALREADY HAVE

When you've got a thousand pounds in your hand, £5 doesn't seem like much does it, but when you've only got £5 and that is all you've got, all of a sudden £5 becomes much more valuable.

You spend it wisely don't you? You'll get a 30p packet of biscuits instead of a £1.85 deluxe packet and you'll buy one stamp for a letter, instead of a book of 12, because that one stamp is all you need.

You become more sensible and thrifty when you have nothing, or very little.

There is so much we take for granted in day to day life.

A few weeks ago I was at the end of my soap, and as I looked at it I began to wonder just how many people would have just thrown it away and started a new one.

With that in mind, I decided to carry on using it until it was no longer possible to use any more and do you know what? I managed to get at least another week out of it! This made me think.

I buy soap in packs of three, which is 12 packs a year. That's nine months of washing! Nine months of soap, that would more than likely be thrown away by many.

The thing is, if you only had that one little bit of soap, that little bit of soap would mean the world to you and would all of a sudden become very precious. This means that you would be forced to get as much out of that soap as possible.

The same applies to toilet roll.

If you were down to your last three sheets, then you wouldn't sit there yanking yards off the roll. You would be very careful, making sure that those last three, were sufficient for you to complete the job in hand (so to speak).

The other day we almost ran out of teabags. We actually had just the one left, but do you know what? That one teabag was enough. I was able to make two cups of tea easily.

This meant that I didn't have to deprive my wife of her cup, because there was plenty for the both of us.

Can you imagine implementing this throughout the year? I worked it out and it would save us at least 1,920 teabags! That's a saving of £31.20 over the twelve months.

Now I'm not suggesting that you all suddenly become scrooges of the year, I'm just pointing out that everything we use, or have, is precious and even though you may think you have nothing at times, you have in fact got much more than enough to get by.

Appreciating what you have in life is very important.

Take a car for instance.

Driving a brand-new Mercedes, or a top of the range BMW is of course very nice and although you probably wouldn't be seen dead in a twenty-year-old Ford Fiesta, I can guarantee that you would really appreciate and treasure that old Ford, if ever you found yourself without a car at all.

The same applies if you've got a Ford Fiesta and suddenly find that you have to start catching the bus, something that you thought you would never have to do in life. If this does happen though, embrace it, appreciate the walk and then enjoy the bus ride…

I always look for the positives in life and always appreciate.

Someone said to me once that her sister had had some really bad luck. She had fallen down the stairs and broken her leg.

"Don't you mean she's been lucky?" I said

"What do you mean?" the woman replied, confused.

I told her that she had been lucky, because she could have broken her two legs, or even worse her back OR even died!

Suddenly her outlook changed. A negative had been turned into a positive. What a lucky sister she had.

WHY WEARING SKINNY JEANS CAN KILL YOU

There's been a health warning on the news today. Apparently wearing skinny jeans is dangerous.

Medical experts have warned that wearing skinny jeans can damage muscles and nerves. They have called it Compartment Syndrome

The report said that a 35-year-old woman, had to be cut out of a pair after her calves ballooned.

I'd just like to point out that the picture in the article is of a slim model, complete with a gorgeous looking bottom and is wearing a perfectly fitting pair of jeans.

This Kate Moss lookalike as far as I could see, was definitely NOT suffering from any kind of Compartment Syndrome whatsoever.

If she'd been a 20-stone woman with a backside the size of a Number 11 bus, struggling to squeeze into a pair of size tens, on the other hand, then it would have made a lot more sense, but this model seemed quite contented, as she lay there sparked out on a big thick rug, daintily pointing her little firm bottom towards the ceiling fan.

To be honest, the article made the serious condition of Compartment Syndrome sound less serious than it actually is.

Compartment Syndrome can be life-threatening and can sometimes happen following surgery to either a damaged or blocked blood vessel.

It can also happen if you are wearing a plaster cast and the swelling from your injury is still going on.

The thing is, even though Compartment Syndrome can be serious, I very much doubt nipping out to Sainsbury's in a pair of Levi's or Wranglers, is going to cause you any major problems.

Another report recently gave out a stark warning to men too.

Wear tight jeans and you could seriously run the risk of twisted testicles!

This time the report shows the picture of a male model, posing in a perfectly fitting pair of jeans and wearing a nice pastel shirt. 'Was this a medical health warning' I thought, or was I looking at the latest 2017 Matalan catalogue?

The thing is, if your testicles were twisted, I very much doubt that you would be posing next to a speedboat, smiling with a glass of champagne in your hand.

A man holding onto his crotch in excruciating pain, I think would have been much more appropriate. At least then we might even think about taking the article a bit more seriously.

I don't know about you, but I tend to notice if my testicles are under any sort of strain. I kind of know what is comfortable and what isn't. As far as I'm concerned, if you wear tight jeans and you want to cut off your crown jewels' blood supply, then it's your own look out and nobody else's.

Have you heard about body shapers?

Body shapers are all the rage at the moment. They're a bit like modern day corsets. They flatten out all the lumps and bobbles to make you look and feel more like Victoria Beckham, instead of looking like a lump of lard.

These products have also been in the news as a possible health risk. This is not my main concern though.

My main concern is for the poor bloke who asked this very girl out on a date six months earlier, only to find out that the girl with the Victoria Beckham figure, is in fact Victoria Bigun, with a figure more like Giant Haystacks.

And this is the problem isn't it?

Your body shaper secret is hidden away while you've got your clothes on, but the time will come, when you decide to strut your stuff on some sun-kissed beach, in a skimpy bikini and that is when there is nowhere to hide. Everything goes pear-shaped and in more ways than one.

This is where your boyfriend finally does a disappearing act, as he tries to fathom out just where his girlfriend went and how the hell Big Daddy ended up on holiday with him.

Body shaper women will be undeterred by this though, as their tortured Victoria Bigun bodies, will struggle on, causing further nerve damage, digestive problems and breathing difficulties.

At the end of the day though, it's all about common sense again isn't it?

If you find that you can't breathe, then loosen your tie, if your feet hurt, then change your shoes, if your shirt won't do up, then get a bigger one AND most importantly of all, if your jeans are too tight, then rush yourself off to A&E.

WHY I THINK EXERCISING IS BAD FOR YOU

Who exercises? Who goes to the gym? Who runs a lot? If yes, then why?

As far as I'm concerned, there are much better ways to look after your body.

Why run for 20 minutes every day, risking the probabilities of a knee operation further on down the line? Why put your body under all that strain and pressure?

It's like driving a car… You've only got so many miles on the clock, before you'll need new tyres and a service. At some point, if you drive it too much something will wear out, and in time it will need repairing or replacing and your body is no different to that.

Exercising should be carried out by taking a nice gentle, but brisk, walk. An exercise that is enjoyable and is joint friendly.

You'll find that people who partake in this kind of exercise are very often happier people. They will smile, they will say hello and they will merrily get on with their business, because they are enjoying it.

Runners on the other hand never smile and very often look like they've just been shot. This is because they are in pain and getting no pleasure out of it at all.

It surely cannot be natural to go tear-arsing round the streets for miles, while at the same time putting yourself through all that grief?

Life should be all about taking it easy, at a nice steady pace. Any other way and your body won't thank you for it, I assure you.

Too much running can cause you all kinds of problems and knees can suffer terribly.

Even when runners start to get knee pain, they still continue to torture themselves.

You see them running along the main road, red faced and sweaty, with a Tubigrip strapped on each knee, obviously in pain, but determined to carry on relentless, because they think running is good for you. Basically, you're just wearing yourself out and in time, your joints will just pack up.

To me, it stands to reason that any big physical exercise is not going to do you any good.

Cycling is supposed to be a great way of exercising, but I disagree. It's fine if you're going to tootle around a country lane for ten minutes, followed by a nice relaxing five minutes sitting by a stream, but constant pedalling for miles, just cannot be good for you at all, especially your hips.

It's like everything else… If you are constantly using something, in time it's simply just going to stop working.

Another thing that happens when you partake in strenuous exercise is the strain that you're putting your heart through.

Just think about it... One minute you're sitting at home reading a book, quite content as you leisurely lean over to feed the goldfish and the next minute you're belting down the High Street like a complete lunatic, with your heart going like the clappers. That just can't be right can it?

Yes, at the end of the day you do need exercise, but exercise that is carried out in a nice relaxed way and not in a way, where you are pushing your body to the limits AND running your mileage up in the process... Go for a walk!

THEY DON'T WANT WORK DO THEY?

"They don't want work do they?"

You will usually hear that phrase, when someone decides they no longer want to do a job they hate, for a pittance of a wage, that won't even pay for their gas and electric.

But if you think about it, why should they?

It's usually said by people who have plenty of money already and don't really understand the plight of so many other's.

Many years ago, you would be able get a job and then stay in that job for life.

If by any chance a company needed to lay people off, they would either ask for voluntary redundancies, or just pick out the redundant jobs. Either way, the workers would be guaranteed a fair few grand and then would more than likely walk straight back into another job.

It's all very different now of course, with everyone on zero hour and short-term contracts. It's very much a hire and fire mentality within the work place. It's now a world where you can find yourself working in a burger bar one day and sitting at home watching *Loose Women* the next.

Work shouldn't be looked at as something you should strive to do anyway.

People are pressured too much into thinking that they should be working towards work.

My son is coming to the end of his 'education' now and I am constantly being asked if he knows what he's going to do.

The thing is, why should he do anything anyway? He'll decide in his own time, IF in fact he wants to do anything at all.

The trouble is, young people are made to believe that they need to make a choice. They are pressured into choosing something that will ultimately send them off down a path that very often ends in misery and boredom.

Why should they do that though? Following their dream is much more important than getting bogged down in the work ethic.

Even if you're not sure what your dream is, just hang on for it, because at some point it will turn up.

Life is about enjoying yourself, not stuck in a job you hate, so if you can float along doing things you enjoy, then do it, because if you don't, you could end up drudging your way through life, until the day you die.

I don't blame people for not wanting to work in a system that is slowly becoming a two-tier pay structure for the majority.

The living wage and the minimum wage is seen as a good thing by so many, but it's a complete disaster as far as I'm concerned.

The problem is companies are forced to pay the minimum wage and are encouraged to pay the living wage. This obviously sets a precedent everywhere, which results in the obvious conclusion. Everyone in time, will be on either one or the other, working in a job that the system thinks they should be doing, just to pay the bills.

No one should ever look down on anyone who decides that they no longer want work, because at the end of the day… Who really does?

MAKE UP YOUR OWN LISTS

If the washing up needs doing, or there are clothes that need hanging up, you can guarantee that my wife will either be up the loft sorting out a box of something or other from 1989, or she'll be in the bathroom cleaning some wall tiles that are situated in a cupboard, that no one can see anyway.

These are jobs that she obviously thinks need doing, but when you've got what looks like three months of washing-up scattered all over the kitchen, half a dozen bathroom tiles hiding in a cupboard, suddenly becomes less of a priority to me.

The main reason she is doing this (apart from being totally disorganised and she obviously doesn't like washing-up) is that her head is cluttered up with unimportant trivial things, things that don't really matter, which lead to doing things that don't really need doing.

This is the problem with most people.

We create long lists of things to do, which are very often pointless anyway, which results in people wasting lots of valuable time in the process.

What you need to do is declutter. Get rid of pointless stuff and live as simple as possible, because doing this will enable you to do exactly what you really want to do in life.

Life is full of trivial things. Things that keep us all busy, but in the grand scheme of things, most of what we do on a day to day basis, doesn't really matter at all.

You need to draw up a list of everything you don't want to do in life and slowly delete them. Every day cross one out and say,

"I'm not doing that again," and replace it with something that you do want to do.

I've got a friend who hasn't got any lists of his own. He just lives a life of doing exactly what his wife wants him to do, even though he doesn't want to do them. He lives his life by his wife's list and not his own.

He doesn't like *The X Factor*, but he watches it anyway, because his wife wants him to watch it with her.

To make things worse, he is forced to watch *The Xtra Factor* as well on ITV2, so, all in all, taking into account the 12 years the programme has been on, he's actually wasted over three years of his life, doing something, that he absolutely hates.

He also hates *Britain's Got Talent*, *I'm a Celebrity Get Me Out of Here*, *The Voice* and all the other programmes that go with them, but he still watches them all, because his wife wants him to, and so the months and years of wasting valuable time builds up and his life slowly ticks away. His whole life has become stagnant, as he just sits and vegetates.

Just think about what he could be doing, instead of sitting staring at a screen every day, just because someone else wants him to.

Life is too short... Don't waste it.

WHY DO WE DO THAT?

You're sitting in a theatre with twelve hundred other people, watching a wonderful performance by new up and coming comedian 'Jimmy Lightfoot', when suddenly it draws to an end and the curtain begins to fall.

You then witness a very strange human activity. Everyone starts banging the ends of their arms together. So what's all that about then?

Things like that fascinate me. Why not feet, knees, elbows, or why anything at all? Why is there a need to bang or clap anything?

New Year's Eve is another one. We wait around for hours just so that we can all stand in a circle and sing a song together. A song that nobody sings at any other time of the year.

Sometimes we'll even sing it with complete strangers. This is of course finished off with a cheer and the customary banging the ends of our arms together again, but why? Why do we do these things?

It's because we follow the crowd. We've been told that this is what we should do every New Year's Eve.

Why not frog march up and down waving our arms about though? Why not stand on one leg with a pair of underpants on our heads? Why not just sit around and do nothing? I'd prefer to do that to be honest. Standing in a circle singing a song with a load of strangers is forced fun as far as I'm concerned. It's forced fun and it should be avoided.

There's a lot of forced fun created by silly follow-the-crowd type activities.

Another is tossing the pancake. Tossing the pancake! What's all that about? Why not just turn it over?

We can't do that though can we, because it's custom to toss it? We must toss it, but only once a year though.

Isn't it strange? We can go 12 months without the slightest mention of a pancake, but as soon as the big day draws near, we go pancake crazy.

I saw an article recently called 'How to Perfectly Toss a Pancake, Without Using a Spatula' Isn't it just a lot easier to use a spatula though? Why do we have to make it into a challenge? Just turn the thing over!

I was interested to find out the origins of Pancake Day, so I decided to have a delve.

I was interested to find out that it was originally a way of using up all the rich foods before Lent, such as eggs, lard and sugar. This was then followed up with a 40-day health regime.

Who does that now though?

For many people pancakes are probably the healthiest thing they'll eat all year anyway, so what's the point? Their yearly pancake has just simply become an addition to their usual diet of pop, chocolate and chips.

There are many things in life that make me wonder just why on earth we do them.

Another one is the way we dress. Why does it matter?

Why is it that you can nip out to the shops for a loaf of bread wearing a casual pair of jeans, but it's frowned upon if you go to a business meeting like it? Do the latter and you will be expected to ditch the jumper and jeans and throw on a suit and tie instead, but why? Why does wearing a suit and having a long piece of thin cloth wrapped around your neck, make you a good business man?

What if an unknown Richard Branson walked into a job interview, dressed in a chicken outfit and pink fluffy slippers? I presume that he'd be shown the door and told never to return. The smart-looking thicko in a suit would get the job every time, wouldn't he?

I think you should be able to wear whatever makes you feel comfortable as a person, within reason obviously. Turning up with a pair of underpants on your head is probably taking it a bit too far and even the chicken outfit is pushing it, but at the end of the day, the way someone dresses should not matter.

This brings me on to the subject of getting dressed for bed.

Sometimes when I get home late in the afternoon, I'll jump into a pair of pyjamas and then throw on a thick cosy dressing gown.

This really baffles my wife, as she can't really understand why anyone would want to do this, especially at five o'clock in the afternoon, but why not? Is there any particular reason why I have to sit around all night, waiting to put them on?

Some people will change into joggers when they get home, but why get changed twice?

Anyway, I've just decided what I'm going to do on New Year's Eve.

When everyone's singing 'Auld Lang Syne', I'm going to sit in the corner, in my pyjamas, quietly munching on an un-tossed pancake.